Wonderlust

Other Titles of Interest from St. Augustine's Press

Michael Davis, *The Poetry of Philosophy: On Aristotle's* Poetics

Aristotle, *Aristotle – On Poetics* (translated by Seth Benardete and Michael Davis)

Leo Strauss, *Xenophon's Socrates*

Leo Strauss, *Xenophon's Socratic Discourse: An Interpretation of the* Oeconomicus

Seth Benardete, *Achilles and Hector: The Homeric Hero*

Seth Benardete, *Herodotean Inquiries*

Seth Benardete, *Sacred Transgressions: A Reading of Sophocles'* Antigone

Ronna Burger, *The Phaedo: A Platonic Labyrinth*

Joseph Cropsey, *Polity and Economy: With Further Thoughts on the Principles of Adam Smith*

Stanley Rosen, *Nihilism: A Philosophical Essay*

Stanley Rosen, *The Ancients and the Moderns: Rethinking Modernity*

Stanley Rosen, *Plato's Symposium*

Stanley Rosen, *Plato's Sophist*

Stanley Rosen, *Plato's Statesman*

Plato, *The Symposium of Plato: The Shelley Translation* (translated by Percy Bysshe Shelley)

Rémi Brague, *Eccentric Culture: A Theory of Western Civilization*

James V. Schall, s.j.., *The Sum Total of Human Understand*

Roger Scruton, *An Intelligent Person's Guide to Modern Culture*

Roger Scruton, *On Hunting*

Roger Scruton, *The Meaning of Conservatism*

Josef Pieper, *Leisure, the Basis of Culture*

Josef Pieper, *Enthusiasm and Divine Madness: On the Platonic Dialogue* Phaedrus

Ian S. Ross, ed., *On the Wealth of Nations: Contemporary Responses to Adam Smith*

John Reeder, ed., *On Moral Sentiments: Contempoary Responses to Adam Smith*

La Rochefoucauld, *Maxims*. Translated by Stuart D. Warner and Stéphane Douard

Robert B. Heywood, ed., *The Works of the Mind*

Otto Bird and Katharine Bird, *From Witchery to Sanctity: The Religious Vicissitudes of the Hawthornes*

WONDERLUST
Ruminations on Liberal Education

MICHAEL DAVIS

ST. AUGUSTINE'S PRESS
South Bend, Indiana
2006

Manufactured in the United States of America.

1 2 3 4 5   11 10 09 08 07 06

Library of Congress Cataloging in Publication Data
Davis, Michael, 1947–
    Wonderlust: ruminations on liberal education / Michael
    Davis. – 1st ed.
        p. cm.
    ISBN 1-58731-935-7 (hardcover : alk. paper)
    1. Education – Philosophy. 2. Education, Humanistic.
    I. Title.
    LB14.7.D39 2005
    370.112 – dc22   2005005591

∞ *The paper used in this publication meets the minimum requirements of the
American National Standard for Information Sciences – Permanence of Paper for
Printed Materials, ANSI Z39.48–1984.*

St. Augustine's Press
www.staugustine.com

For my students

Table of Contents

ACKNOWLEDGMENTS

I am indebted to a number of people for help with this book. I especially want to thank April Reynolds Mosolino, who pestered me over the years to find a way to reach a broader audience for the many talks I had given when she was a student at Sarah Lawrence College. She heard the first chapter as a lecture welcoming her incoming freshman class to college and the final chapter as a lecture honoring the departure of the same class upon its graduation. And by now, she is quite familiar with all those in between. Susan Johnson carefully read through the entirety of the manuscript and proposed valuable revisions. Several other people also read all or parts of it and made useful comments. Still others invited me to give the talks that eventually developed into the chapters of this book. I want to thank Robert Berman, Ronna Burger, David Blankenship, David and Mary Nichols, Bradd Shore, Richard Velkley, and Stuart Warner. I am grateful as well to Sarah Lawrence College for having been the sort of place that asked me to give talks like these and to Bruce Fingerhut for running the sort of press that is interested in publishing them. Sarah Lawrence also generously provided me with two grants to assist in preparing the manuscript for publication. Two of the chapters appeared previously in print (chapter nine in the first issue of *Ancient Philosophy* in the fall of 1980 and chapter twelve in *Perspectives on Political Science* in the winter of 2003). Finally, I want to thank my wife, Susan Heldt Davis, who has always been my first audience and, because she is able to take me seriously while never losing her sense of fun, also my most honest audience.

PREFACE

This little book is not meant to be yet another defense of liberal education – although I much admire such defenses. It was born of aspirations less grand. It seeks neither to be morally edifying nor to avoid the fact that education cannot be understood apart from the question of morality. My hope is rather to say something useful about the nature of education, for education has at its heart something difficult to articulate. Arid learning, moral posturing, antiquarian curiosity, revolutionary theorizing, self-aggrandizing casuistry – these are more familiar to us. Education wouldn't be necessary if the nature of things were perfectly manifest. And it wouldn't be possible if the nature of things were altogether obscure and unavailable. Only because we are so immersed in a world whose nature is imperfectly clear to us can we pose questions at all. We know and at the same time do not know. In part, our situation was nicely described by Pascal: "We know too little to be dogmatists and too much to be skeptics." But were this the complete story, ours might be a tragedy – we would be situated in a world we long to know, knowing only enough to know that we do not and cannot finally know. Fortunately, something relieves us of this burden. Without the expectation of an answer, the act of questioning is unintelligible. At the same time, when, in the middle of an informal conversation, we introduce a question with the words "I wonder. . . .", it is not clear that we really want an immediate and definitive answer. "I wonder" is an opening move – an invitation to begin an inquiry, to think through a problem. And it often involves playfully calling into question something that we have not yet seriously doubted. The fact is that wondering about things – ruminating – is deeply pleasant. We have much to learn from Plato and Aristotle, both of whom saw that philosophy originates in wonder and that philosophy is in some sense at the core of our humanity. One might say that giving wonder its due is the acid test for liberal education. It would involve the hard-nosed insistence that learning be more than self-indulgent talk without succumbing to the pseudo-toughness of learning as job preparation. The wonder test is hard to administer, however, for its results are easily aped. A little book would earn its keep if it gave some help in administering the test.

Aristotle remarks in his *Metaphysics* that the question of being was, is, and always will be perplexing.[1] He seems to mean, among other things, that we will never be able to roll up our sleeves, look under the hood and solve this most fundamental philosophic question so as to bequeath its solution to future generations. Metaphysical questions, at least, are perennial, and, since what holds for the question of being holds for all questions (not that we cannot think them through, perhaps even solve them, but that whatever life their answers have depends on preserving within them the process that gave rise to them), in the deepest sense thinking requires that we always start over from the beginning. We never get to stand on the shoulders of previous generations because genuine ideas arise only from genuine questions. Inherited ideas are like clichés – once striking but for that very reason repeated so often that they have lost the power they once had to cause us to think. "Rational animal" may be the most powerful description ever put forth of human beings, but without rethinking what led Aristotle to it, we are left with a bare formula – a shadow of an idea. All ideas are therefore somehow new to the one who thinks them. To recover the power of a dead metaphor is to think it anew. Because genuine education requires an unending renewal of wonder in the face of the inevitable erosion of complacency, it must be profoundly revolutionary.

At the same time, it would be strange if any idea were really new. The circumstances of our lives certainly change from

1   See *Metaphysics* 1028b.

generation to generation. Human beings are obviously treated more equally in certain ages and places than in others, and yet the idea of human equality was understood as radically by Plato and Aristotle as by any contemporary thinker. The questions that we put to the world are ordinarily generated out of everyday concerns. Equality, for example, is likely to be a more immediate issue in a democracy than in an aristocracy. Aristotle calls these issues what is "first to us." In this sense every age begins thinking with its own idiosyncratic problems. But to deepen our thoughts means to pare away this idiosyncrasy so as to articulate the core of our perplexity in terms that are not peculiar to our time and place. Aristotle calls this what is "first by nature." Thinking consists in moving from what is wondrous because new (what is first to us) to what is simply wondrous (what is first by nature). Wherever there have been human beings they have wondered about their world. Accordingly, it seems unlikely that the deepest thoughts of the deepest thinkers are not connected to common questions. In this sense an altogether new idea is likely to be superficial – "first to us" and not "first by nature." Because genuine education requires an unending retrieval of what is in principle always knowable, in rejecting the complacency of the "new," it must be profoundly conservative.

For us, the impassioned defense of liberal education has recently largely taken the form of a defense of the tradition of the West. This defense has a curious duality. On the one hand, it is a call to preserve the noble ideals of the Western World, invoking, among other things, Jerusalem and Athens, the Roman Republic, the Renaissance, and Magna Carta. It claims the best that has been thought, written, imaged, and composed as our inheritance from a civilization now at risk – a civilization which, once lost, will give way to a new barbarism. This defense is moral and political. Its liberal education has a positive content and is concerned in large measure with preserving the conditions for human liberty. It would be fair to state its end as civic virtue. And it would be foolish to dismiss it. Still, there is another defense of liberal education according to which its end is to free us from thoughtless and ingrained opinions, from our tendency to see the world in a fixed way, and so to encourage us to wonder about what we have most taken for granted. Its liberal education is essentially intellectual and philosophical. Some years ago Allan Bloom wrote a famously successful paean to liberal education, *The Closing of the American Mind*. Bloom, more than familiar with Plato's *Apology of Socrates* as the *locus classicus* of the problem of the relation between moral and philosophical education, was surely aware that his title vividly points to the tension between these two defenses. Is the goal of liberal education to open minds or to educate Americans? Can an open mind be an American mind?

Philosophy too has its curious duality. On the one hand it is received wisdom – according to Alfred North Whitehead, "a series of footnotes to Plato."[2] Studying philosophy of this sort means learning a tradition of thought about certain fundamental questions. On the other hand, philosophy is a way of life, the habit of having no habits, and involves a fixed disposition to question and to expose opinion for what it is – mere opinion. *Philosophia* is the *love* of wisdom; it is only owing to our lack of wisdom that we can want it. But we never start from nothing. It is our natural condition to have conventions – opinions that we believe to be true – which we hold most firmly when we do not realize that we hold them at all, when they shape our world behind our backs. Beginning from these unconfirmed opinions, philosophy as a way of life seeks to transform them into knowledge. Of course all opinions are not equal. Some involve matters more important to us than others. Philosophy as a way of life is thus an attempt to get at the truth about what is important, what concerns us most, what is good. Philosophy as a way of life thus has two overriding questions: What is true? and What is good? This pair, in turn, suggests a third: What is the connection between the true and the good?

Students go off to college and their parents remain at home, both in a state of uncomfortable, if healthy, confusion about the goals of education. On the one hand there is a not unreasonable expectation that education involves learning something. In a crude sense this shows up as anxiety about the future. Students, and their parents, sometimes view education as job training. But the expectation that

2 Alfred North Whitehead, *Process and Reality*, (New York: Free Press, 1969), 53.

education will fill us with content has more subtle manifestations as well. Very earnest students sometimes want to study Greek philosophy because it seems necessary to them to start at the beginning if they are to master the subsequent tradition. But if Plato and Aristotle are understood as building blocks – parts of a foundation – then the building is what is being investigated, and Plato and Aristotle are never really understood in their own terms. That they might simply teach us something true is not really considered. Early in my career, before I learned that teaching does not always involve saying everything that you think when you think it, an enthusiastic and intelligent freshmen in an introductory course came to me to discuss her first paper. It was on Aristophanes' play, *The Clouds*. I had asked the class to tell me why the play was called *The Clouds*, which was really to ask why Aristophanes had written a play about philosophy in which he creates a chorus of clouds as gods. My student, a good student, came to meet me with a dozen books under her arm – about Aristophanes, Socrates, Greek history, etc. She was doing research. I told her to take the books back to the library. She dropped the course. For her, thinking still meant collecting. I did not yet realize that my job was not to tell her but to teach her where to begin.

The other pole of this confusion about education is liberation – from parents, from fixed curricula, from the dreary business of establishing a resume appropriate to get yourself into a good college, and, of course, from answers to questions that have never adequately been asked. Man is a political animal according to Aristotle because he can only realize his nature within political life. We learn to behave according to certain standards of good and bad within the family, but it is in the *polis*, the political community, that we must articulate these standards. Even the behavior of animals is teleological; they aim at certain goods. But it is human beings who in saying to themselves "this is good" mean that it is good for all and so first think in terms of justice and injustice.

College, on the one hand a place for the reverent study of traditional and authoritative sources of wisdom, is on the other hand a place for the irreverent questioning of authority. It is not easy to balance these two requirements, and most institutions will err on one side or the other. Over thirty years ago as a graduate student in

Germany I attended a seminar by Hans-Georg Gadamer. He was already at that time famous – known not only as the premier student of Martin Heidegger but as a thinker in his own right. The seminar was about evenly divided between Germans and foreign students; of the latter the majority were Americans. The German students were meticulously respectful, always asking very small, well planned, specific questions that had the character of footnotes to the overall interpretation of Plato's *Philebus* that Gadamer was laying out. The American students – on the whole far more brash, less careful, less concerned about the details, less well-prepared, and in general less educated and more full of themselves – were also on the whole more interesting. They asked things they really had no business asking, and were for that reason more radical and so more philosophical. The ideal student would know as much as the Germans and be as free-wheeling as the Americans, would, in Seth Benardete's memorable phrase, "surrender to authority while fighting all the way."[3]

Doing justice to the demands of genuine thinking would mean teaching to this ideal student. It would be at once moral and philosophical, conservative and revolutionary. But in doing justice to the good, it would never forsake the true. It would approach the tradition with enormous respect by demanding that it shed light on the pressing questions of contemporary life. At the same time it would do justice to the richness of ordinary life by expecting day-to-day experience to have deep philosophical implications. The slightly off humor of a Gary Larson cartoon can teach us something about Aristotle's *Metaphysics*. The enormous significance of the execution of Socrates by the city of Athens has echoes in the question of the imposition of speech codes in the contemporary university. In the day-to-day life of an undergraduate college there are a variety of occasions that call for reflecting on the nature of a liberal arts education – orientations and graduations, to be sure, but also panel discussions and talks to groups of students. Such times are especially rich opportunities to make manifest the close connection between philosophy and everyday life. They force us to reflect on our lives as rational animals as wholes. Most of the essays that follow were orig-

3 "Interpreting Plato's *Charmides*" in *The Argument of the Action*, 243.

inally lectures for such occasions; they were composed over a period of thirty years while teaching at several undergraduate colleges, but primarily at Sarah Lawrence College. Since this is meant to be a book about the intimacy and the necessity of both the bond and the tension between the particularity peculiar to life and the universality of thought, I have chosen to retain some of the informality of style appropriate to occasional pieces while indicating the character of the occasion by way of footnotes.

In a way I mean this to be a very practical book written for students and their parents. It is oddly ironic that as the cost of undergraduate education soars, we find it increasingly difficult to articulate what it is really for. There can be no easy answer to this question, for to solve it we would have to know what human beings are for, and that is surely a lifetime's work. Still, it is possible to get a feel for the sorts of questions that need to come up if a college is doing its work. It is with this end in mind that I have thought it worthwhile to publish these ruminations on liberal education.

Part One

LIBERAL EDUCATION AND EXPERIENCE

Chapter 1

FREEDOM AND RESPONSIBILITY[1]

About two and a half months ago the Dean asked me to give this talk on "freedom and responsibility." I didn't have to ask her what she had in mind; the topic is a dead give-away. When I ran into the Associate Dean on campus a month later, he asked me for a title. I said, "I don't know. How about 'Freedom and Responsibility'?" He responded with "How about 'Freedom and Responsibility at Sarah Lawrence'?" This was an even deader give-away. College Deans think like parents, but can't afford to admit it to themselves because they have to consider you responsible adults – free agents. My daughter, Jessica, is leaving for college this fall – actually the day after tomorrow. My wife and I decided last June that Jessica probably shouldn't have a curfew any longer. She was eighteen, about to go off on her own and, if old enough to vote for president, ought to be able to decide what time to come in at night. Jessica was pleased to hear this of course, but knew that she was also about to get "the speech." We wanted her to know that this was not license to start staying out until all hours. We expected her to behave responsibly. This is parental code for "We don't want to tell you what to do; we only want you to do exactly what we would have told you to do had we told you – which we didn't." This is called freedom. Once

1 First presented as a Freshman Orientation Address at Sarah Lawrence College, August 1993.

explained, it is not nearly as much fun as it was supposed to have been. Now, the Deans wouldn't think of restricting your freedom; they just want you to be responsible, i.e., act as they think you should. Yet I don't want to be too hard on them. I'm sure that God felt the same way on the sixth day of the creation.

Freedom and responsibility are a problematic pair. Everyone begins with a sense that the two do not go together. This is clearer if one substitutes the word duty for responsibility. It is not with an airy feeling of liberation that one does one's duty. Duty is heavy; freedom is light. Accordingly Jacob Klein remarks that chains seem to be the universal symbol of freedom.[2] The statue in New York Harbor could represent any number of noble things; only when labeled does it become the Statue of Liberty. But a statue of someone throwing off chains would have needed no label. We first experience freedom as a removal of constraint; a weight lifts from us. This happens to me after I've finished writing something. I celebrate by clearing off my desk; it is a sign that there is no longer anything I have to do. So rather than being connected to responsibility, freedom initially seems to mean the possibility of being irresponsible, unconnected to anything whatsoever. It is play, not work.

And yet there is nothing less serious than play. You have all seen advertisements of the young and beautiful running through a field (to sell cigarettes), or playing volleyball on the beach (to sell beer), or cavorting in a playground at 3 AM or generally behaving like idiots, or, more charitably, like children (although no children I know would be caught dead behaving in this way). These people are free, where "free" means altogether uninhibited and without thought of consequences; they live in the moment for no purpose apart from it.

But what would it really mean to live with no thought of consequences? William Faulkner wrote a novel called *Go Down Moses*. Its title is on the one hand a reference to an African-American spiritual, and so to racial slavery in the United States, and on the other to the Biblical account of the enslavement of the Jews in Egypt. In

---

2   Jacob Klein, lecture presented at *The Aspen Institute for Humanistic Studies* (1952).

either case, the issue is slavery, and hence freedom. In the very middle of this book on freedom Faulkner begins a chapter called "The Bear," and in the very middle of "The Bear" is a conversation between Isaac (Ike) McCaslin and his cousin McCaslin (Cass) Edmunds. Ike has inherited an estate established by his grandfather Caruthers McCaslin who "bought" it rather unscrupulously from Indians, built it up on the backs of slaves, had a daughter by one of those slaves and another by committing incest with this daughter. Caruthers McCaslin was not a forebear to be proud of. Ike, wanting nothing to do with this legacy, plans to repudiate his title to the land. Cass, who will become the owner in his stead, urges him to keep the land. To surrender it means simply to give it up to another who will not use it as well as Ike would have. The argument between them is ultimately about what it means for us, who are immersed in a temporal order, to be free. If we are what we are by virtue of what produced us, can we ever simply repudiate this past? And if not, can we ever truly act freely?

Let's begin again. If freedom means anything, it surely must mean that I can have an effect in the world. I can intend to do something and watch it happen as a result of my intention. I can be a cause. The Greek word for cause is *aition*; as an adjective, it means responsible. To be free means to act in such a way as to be responsible for the way things turn out. I cannot cut myself off from what I do; the unconnected gratuitous act that seems so spontaneous and whimsical doesn't really exist. Human beings can never live in the present. When we call people responsible we are therefore only calling attention to what all human beings must be if they are to be causes and so free. The only question is whether they acknowledge it.

Now, if freedom meant at any moment being able to do whatever we wanted, we would have to at any moment be able to extricate ourselves from the chain of effects we had produced at a previous moment. Nothing we did before could have any effect on what we were about to do. At each moment we would begin anew, cutting ourselves free from responsibility for what we had previously done. Of course, looking ahead, whatever we were about to do would quickly become one of these disowned past deeds. In other words, if

we are to understand ourselves as causes, we cannot understand ourselves as utterly free causes because we never begin from an
absolute beginning point. If our present actions were not to emerge
out of our previous actions, they would not emerge as ours at all. If
freedom means that at any moment anything is possible, then nothing we do makes any difference whatsoever. Complete freedom
would be purchased at the price of the utter meaninglessness of our
action. But one utterly meaningless action is altogether indistinguishable from another; if I were completely free I could, therefore,
not really do anything. My freedom would be indistinguishable from
blind chance. Genuine freedom would seem to be inseparable from
responsibility.

But wait, let's start over again. Many years ago I had a conversation with my mother in which she was bemoaning something that
my sister had done, something that seemed terrible to her at the time
(now it seems relatively trivial). At one point my mother uttered the
classic parental plaint – "What did I do wrong?" I remember telling
her that she really couldn't blame herself, since if she were responsible for the terrible thing my sister had done then her own mother
(my grandmother) should be held responsible for everything she
(my mother) did, including whatever terrible thing she had done to
my sister to make her do such a terrible thing. You get the point. To
be free means to be a cause, to initiate events that are part of a chain.
But what exempts us from being a part of this chain? I cannot be free
unless I think of myself as responsible, and yet the conditions under
which I can be responsible make what I do part of a chain of events
of which I cannot simply understand myself to be the initiator. To
claim responsibility seems to be possible only under conditions that
ultimately make it impossible to claim responsibility.

Speaking of temporal chains, Aristotle had already seen all of
this in the fourth century B.C. In the third book of his *Nicomachean
Ethics* he raises the question of whether virtuous action has to be
voluntary, and concludes that it does; otherwise it is not praisewor-
thy. What then is voluntary action? It is movement that comes from
within and not from the outside. Aristotle examines a number of
puzzling cases. For example, if you are at sea in a storm and in order

to save your life it becomes necessary to throw your cargo over-board, is this action voluntary? Aristotle says yes and no. You do choose to throw the cargo overboard, but you certainly do not choose to be in the middle of a storm. But aren't all choices governed by conditions that were not themselves chosen? Aristotle asks for example whether we choose to be the sorts of beings who are pleased by certain things and pained by others, and find certain things noble and certain things base. Since we don't, and since pleasure and pain and the noble and the base attach themselves as reasons for virtually everything we do, it seems as though no action is truly free. Everything we do is conditioned by the natures we happen to have, and as Wallace Stevens says "Happens to like is one of the ways things happened to fall."[3] Aristotle does a curious thing, however, in his discussion of this issue. He several times raises and backs away from it by changing the subject. He reveals the principle behind this hedging when he says that "if someone should claim the pleasant and the noble are compulsory, all things would thus be compulsory" (1110b9). The problem is that you cannot say the pleasant and noble are compulsory and mean it. To have identified something as pleasant is to have identified it as desirable and so already to have pursued it in your mind, i.e. already to have considered yourself an agent free to choose it. It might be possible for everything to be involuntary, but it is not something one can say and believe.

Let's start again. Throughout his account of the voluntary and the involuntary Aristotle cuts off further discussion when things threaten to get difficult by saying that if nothing were voluntary, not only would it be impossible to blame anyone, for anything it would also be impossible to praise anyone. Now, why couldn't one simply accept this and agree to forego all praise? Nothing is voluntary, and thus no praise is ever justifiable. However, the question of the voluntary and the involuntary comes up in the first place only because we wish to avoid feeling responsible for what is bad. Yet only someone who already feels responsible wishes to escape feeling responsible.

3   Stevens, Wallace, "Table Talk" in *Opus Posthumus* (New York: Knopf, 1957) 40.

To want to say "it's not my fault" is already to have identified yourself as someone whose fault it could be – a responsible agent. This is of course not an argument for human freedom. It means only that, if we are honest with ourselves, we must acknowledge that it is impossible for us to consider ourselves anything other than free.

What have we seen so far? At first, freedom and responsibility seem at odds. Freedom means doing what we wish to do; responsibility means doing what we feel we have to do. But freedom then turns out to be impossible without responsibility. We have really done nothing unless we can claim to be causes of events in the world; feeling free goes hand in hand with accepting responsibility for what we have done. And yet the conditions for responsibility, and hence freedom, end up seemingly at odds with responsibility. How can we ever claim truly to have initiated anything? Are we not simply members of a long line of causes that are each also effects of prior causes? Finally, it turns out that this whole issue cannot even arise for us unless we consider ourselves responsible, and hence free. We are only troubled by the possibility that we are not free because we cannot really consider ourselves anything but free. When you argue that you are not free, don't you hope to convince others on the basis of the evidence you supply? Doesn't this mean that you consider them free to weigh the merits of your argument? If not, then why are you making an argument at all? To argue that we are not free is a subtle attempt to affirm our dignity in a world where we do not feel in control. It is a claim to be free.

Now, someone might reasonably ask whether we haven't simply generated an antinomy in which, regardless of where we start, we will always end up by contradicting our beginning point. I wonder. Perhaps something has been revealed of the structure of our experience of ourselves as free. Freedom begins as rebellion, a declaration of independence *from*. We are the beings who first discover our dignity when we say "you can't do that to me." But this first negative affirmation leads willy-nilly to another. The reason you can't do that to me is that I am a cause in my own right, not simply an object to be used at will. Now, to make my causality intelligible to myself I must think of it in terms of its effects. In doing so, I risk undermining my dignity. To give an explanation for it is after all to give an account of its cause. Still, the deeper purpose of this account is always an affirmation of my dignity. The experience of freedom thus has two moments, one in which I burst the limits imposed on me from without, and another in which I re-impose limits on myself from within.

So far this afternoon I have pretty much gone my own idiosyncratic way. The Dean and the Associate Dean surely did not envision all of this when they asked me to give a talk on freedom and responsibility, let alone freedom and responsibility at Sarah Lawrence. Well, I've always been a little skeptical of orientation anyway. Orientation seems to me to stand to college life as talking about a relationship is to being in love. In both cases the former bears little relation to the latter. Still, as I have my responsibilities, perhaps I should conclude in a more immediately applicable way. The most serious question concerning freedom on college campuses today has to do with freedom of speech. At the outset of your college careers it won't do any harm to caution you to exercise this freedom responsibly. You are not atoms in the void; what you say affects other human beings. But doesn't freedom of speech mean it is permissible to say anything? Isn't the exercise of free speech a virtue in and of itself? And isn't the regulation of speech – speech codes, for example – an insult to your dignity? Or is free speech only truly free when it is exercised responsibly? For the record, I am a long-standing opponent of speech codes on college campuses. I don't believe people ought to be officially punished for offending others in speech. Sometimes people deserve to be offended. Does this mean they should be praised for saying whatever is on their minds? No, freedom doesn't simply mean throwing off all restraint. As we have seen it is necessarily linked to responsibility. What you produce as an action or a speech leads back to you as its cause. If you do or say something contemptible the appropriate response is that you should be held in contempt. This is what it means to be free; if it doesn't mean that, then your speech is altogether meaningless – idle chatter. When we get angry at what others have said we do them the honor of taking them seriously. Your dignity depends not only on being able to do what you wish. It depends also on being praised and blamed for what you do. Yes, you are free to say what you want. But you also need to wonder about where it came from and take responsibility for where it goes after it leaves your mouth.

If this is so, what is wrong with regulating speech – with speech codes? We always need to keep in mind that this is an academic community. Its deepest goal is education – ultimately thinking. Accordingly, we need to be most vigilant in guarding against whatever conflicts with thinking. Presumably you would not be sitting here had you already settled all of the deepest human questions. Now, several times in the course of speaking today I have said something like "let's begin again." It is unfortunately never simply possible to begin again in one's actions. Where we can go is always conditioned by where we have been. Our freedom is of a limited sort. But thoughts are different. Thinking means being able to wipe the slate clean after a false start. This is what makes it possible to think dangerous, unpopular or shocking, but not thereby necessarily false, thoughts. Nothing contingent limits one's freedom of thought, only the truth. This is what is so enchanting about the life of the mind. The question for you, then, when you are offended by someone's speech, is whether the speech is in the service of thought. Laws – speech codes – are notoriously clumsy when it comes to this distinction; so it is up to you. A lot is at stake, for a world in which we all mindlessly say the right thing seems to me an infinitely poorer place than a world where we sometimes offend, but genuinely think. And since the truth often hurts, these are not simply "academic" alternatives.

I want to welcome you to Sarah Lawrence, where there are of course no curfews. But please, try to get a good night's sleep occasionally.

Chapter 2

THE TWO FREEDOMS OF SPEECH IN PLATO[1]

Freedom of speech is like a mantra for us. We regularly invoke it but seldom pause to ask ourselves what we are talking about. I suppose the obvious place to begin – and begin is all one can hope to do here – is by thinking about speech. Speech always has a double function – it articulates and it communicates.[2] Through speech we say one thing is another, but saying X is Y means tacitly asserting the apartness of X and Y. If the two were simply one they would not need to be put together. This is how we make sense of things, analyzing them into parts and seeing how they form parts of larger wholes. The Greek word for speech – one of them at least – is logos. We regularly use it in English in compound words. Biology is the logos of bios, an articulation or making sense of life (bios). But speech is also how we make others aware of what we are thinking or at least what we wish them to think we are thinking. It is an essentially public act insofar as it is designed to influence others – to persuade them. Speech is both philosophic and political. It is probably not accidental that the English word "intention" has a double sense. Speech is our means of intending, where to intend may be either to

1 First presented at the Helen Merrill Lynd Colloquium, Sarah Lawrence College, Spring 1993.
2 Heracleitus noticed this over 2500 years ago (fragment 1).

mean or to will. It is certainly not accidental that Plato's Socrates is the first to call philosophy dialectics. *Dialektikê* is formed from a verb which in its middle voice – *dialegesthai* – means to converse or have dialogue and in its active voice – *dialegein* – means to divide or separate. The noun cognate with this verb is *logos*. Speech is simultaneously the speech of dialogue and the speech of thought. Has this doubleness an analogue on the level of freedom of speech? Is there a political freedom of speech and a philosophical freedom of speech?

Political freedom of speech serves the common good; it is a hedge against tyranny. Political life means living together, not mechanically and thoughtlessly like bees and ants, but with a view to the purpose of our association. It necessarily involves talk among us about what is good and bad. Those who control what we can say will accordingly control the range of purposes permitted to our community. More often than not, being human, they will have in view their own good rather than the common good. Even if they are of good faith, they will unwittingly exclude certain promising possibilities from public consideration. Speaking of the practice of licensing books to permit their publication, Francis Bacon says "authorized.books are but the language of the times."[3] It is rare to be able think anything but the platitudes of one's own age (that it is impossible to do so is one of the platitudes of our age), rarer still, I suspect, among the sort of people who will choose to become censors, who will probably not be thinkers of the deepest thoughts. We ought never to forget that restrictions on freedom of speech must ultimately mean restrictions exercised by some human beings over others. Political freedom of speech, then, is an instrument in the service of the common good. It protects us from narrow thoughts and narrow men.

And yet, as instrumental, it can be only as good as the end it produces and only good insofar as it produces this end. Accordingly it is regularly limited. It may be true that "congress shall make no law . . . abridging freedom of speech," but falsely shouting fire in a

3 In *Areopagitica* Milton quotes this passage from Francis Bacon's *An Advertisement Touching the Controversies of the Church of England.*

crowded theater is far from the only thing we are prohibited to say. When I first started teaching, I went to a dinner party in which the discussion turned to what children ought to be told about death. One of my colleagues said she intended to tell her three-year-old the truth – that after you died you were put in a wooden box and buried under the ground. I kept imagining her child's nightmares. I'm glad she wasn't my mother. Free speech, even when it involves saying the truth as you understand it, is not always such a wonderful thing. The Germans have just outlawed several neo-Nazi groups. Given the history of the twentieth century, do we really want to chastise them for this? Another of our platitudes is that in the marketplace of free ideas, the best will ultimately win out. But why should this be the case, and, even if it were, when will they win out and for how long? A lot of damage can be done while the marketplace is working its magic. Lives have more than once been lost and reputations destroyed beyond repair on the basis of false speech. If freedom of speech is good as an instrument for the realizing of the common good, then when it can be seen to undermine the common good, we can no longer think it simply good. When it is an instrument for slander, inflaming hatred or undermining the very foundation of a community, can it still be said to be in the service of the common good? That it is difficult to decide when the threat to our common good is profound enough to warrant regulating speech by no means releases us from the obligation to decide whether it does. In principle, at least, political freedom of speech is not absolute.

Democratic Athens of the fifth century B.C. prided itself on a degree of freedom of speech unparalleled in the Greek world. Their word for it was formed from *pas*, "everything," and *rhêsis*, "saying"; *parrêsia* means saying everything – its cognate verb, to be frank. In Plato's dialogue *Gorgias*, Socrates holds a conversation about the power of *logos* with Gorgias, the most famous of Greek rhetoricians, followed by a conversation about justice with Polus, Gorgias's student, followed by a conversation about pleasure with Callicles, an upper-class Athenian. Each of them loses his argument because he is at some point shamed into saying something he does not really mean. They each intend something by their speeches that their speeches do not really intend. Although both Polus and Callicles profess to be willing to "say everything," neither is really up to it. Early on in the dialogue Socrates describes himself as even more eager to be refuted by others than to refute them since to be refuted is to be benefited (Socrates is no altruist). Unlike his various interlocutors who have reputations, moral beliefs or idiosyncratic tastes to defend, Socrates presents himself as entering into conversation ready to say anything if only it seems correct to him. He understands his self-interest to be so bound up with learning the truth that victory is of secondary importance. Power to win without really knowing what you want – what's good for you – is not really power. Socrates' "frankness" is rooted in his longing for wisdom – his *parrêsia* is his *philosophia*. Freedom is the necessary and absolute condition for the possibility of the full exercise of speech as articulation – for philosophy. If in trying to figure something out we are constrained by anything other than the *logos*, the logic of our own speech, the result will be tainted. This sort of freedom of speech admits of no compromise and no limitation. Thinking is by nature a great risk; should we promise ourselves in advance only to think decent thoughts, nice thoughts, we will have forsworn it. If we are so repelled by the idea of cannibalism that it calls forth from us only disgust, how can we hope to understand what moved teenage Red Guards to practice it during Mao's Cultural Revolution? And if moral outrage at sexual discrimination causes us to suppress thoughts about the import of the difference between the sexes, the first thing Adam and Eve notice about their world after being thrust out of paradise will be closed off to us as an object of inquiry. Regulating hateful speech may be necessary for the life of a community; it is the death of thought, for, while there are things that are truly hateful, we also tend to hate truths that discomfit us.

There are then two freedoms of speech, one instrumental and contingent, and the other absolute, but the relation between the two is complicated. Frankness is frequently understood as a moral virtue. Aristotle makes *parrêsia* a characteristic of the great-souled man, the man perfectly at home with himself (*Nicomachean Ethics* 1124b29). We too tend to admire sincerity, authenticity and "telling it like it is," even if in our skeptical age this can only mean telling it like it seems. This moral version of freedom of speech as articulation would seem to overcome the tension between the two freedoms; expressing oneself would become not simply a means to communal life but the meaning of communal life. The present age comes perilously close to this alternative, but fortunately common sense overrules our sense of logic; by self-expression we really mean only a variety of forms of "nice" speech. Talk of racial superiority, chauvinism or the thousand year Reich is somehow not thought to be a manifestation of the morality of self-expression. It may be tolerated, but only as a means to a greater end, not as an end in itself. Aristotle was more consistent. It is a virtue in the great-souled to be frank because the great-souled are good. Only because they know what they are talking about can the great-souled "tell it like it is."

On the other hand, there is artistic freedom of expression – for us perhaps the crux of the matter. It has no doubt always been a matter for debate, but it is probably not coincidental that the Inquisition and the inventing of the printing press are coincidental. Because art issues in a product, it always has a public dimension. For artists, speech or expression seems to be articulation – telling it like it seems. At the same time, they of necessity communicate what they articulate. And in an age of mass publication, films, television, etc. – that is, in an age of reproduction – they do so with increasing effect. From the point of view of the artist as artist freedom of expression is the freedom of speech as articulation. To limit it is to annihilate it. Accordingly it seems to have an absolute character. From the point of view of the public who view the product of an artist's expression, however, things look different. The artist's work will have an effect on the health of the body politic, an effect at times potentially so harmful as to warrant censorship. Freedom of speech is, after all, instrumental to the common good. This tension between art and society at large is simply a version of the tension within speech itself between articulation and communication. It could be fully resolved in one of two ways: if artists were to express only what is thought to be the common good or if society at large were to embrace artistic expression as its ultimate purpose. In the first instance art ceases to be art. In the second, the demands of ordinary life – food, shelter, clothing, safety, etc. – make the resolution at best a naive hope based on an untrue view of the relation of life to art. We have interests other than self-expression. It is therefore the business of those who make something like the truth of things their goal, those for whom speech as articulation is primary, to understand the necessity for compromise. The truth of the relation between art as truth-seeking and political life is that they will be forever at odds. The one prides itself on taking nothing for granted, the other cannot exist without taking certain things for granted. The best that can be hoped for is an uneasy truce. Artists have to protect their freedom of expression jealously without becoming overly self-righteous in their condemnation of the necessities of the ordinary lives of ordinary people – they are also, after all, ordinary people.

The title of these remarks is "The Two Freedoms of Speech in Plato." Athens executed Plato's teacher, Socrates, for "corrupting the young and not believing in the gods of the city." The thought that the greatest city of his time could put to death the greatest thinker of his time for his thoughts is the thread that runs through all Platonic philosophy. In Plato's version of his trial, the *Apology of Socrates*, Socrates defends his way of life, philosophy, by saying not very convincingly that a god told him to do it. He then claims that, rather than corrupting the young by undermining conventional standards of virtue, he teaches them virtue, neglecting to point out that the "virtue" he teaches them in fact amounts to the practice of asking what virtue is – philosophy. The *Apology* is a remarkable example of Socratic double-talk, for he succeeds in making clear the absolute claim that philosophy must have over him while at the same time deferring to the conventional "wisdom" – i.e., the prejudices – of his judges. That he submits to the judgment of Athens points in two directions. On the one hand, he takes philosophy seriously enough to die for it. In reply to the possibility that he might be acquitted if he were to give up philosophy Socrates answers, "While I breathe and am able I will not cease from philosophizing" (*Apology* 29d). On the other hand, he takes political life seriously enough to accept his judges' verdict – Socrates had ample opportunity to escape. In defending philosophy without absolutizing the claims of freedom of speech, Socrates provides a model for Plato's turn to political philosophy as the "eccentric core of philosophy."[4] This Socratic understanding of the togetherness of and the tension between philosophy and politics is finally rooted in the doubleness of speech or *logos*, and so of human beings, the animals with *logos*. We could do worse than to look to it as a model for our own understanding of freedom of speech.

One final thing. Freedom of speech has become a trendy issue. Political correctness and speech codes on campus are the hot topics of the day. It might help in thinking through these issues to ask ourselves what an academic community is. If it were a *polis* – an association for the comprehensive human good – a number of limitations on freedom of speech might be justified. However, the deepest goal of the academy is education – ultimately, thinking. More than any other human community, therefore, it needs to preserve the absoluteness of freedom of speech as articulation. For you can only be said to think if there is nothing you dare not think.

---

4 See Seth Benardete, "Leo Strauss' *The City and Man*," *Political Science Reviewer* 8 (1978), 5.

Chapter 3

SPEECH CODES AND
THE LIFE OF LEARNING[1]

For students, a college is ordinarily at least two things – necessarily related but not always altogether compatible. It's a place to live and a place to learn. Accordingly, community regulations have two sorts of justifications – either to assure that the college will be a good place to live or that it will be a good place to learn. I take it for granted that communities can under certain circumstances regulate speech. In some opinion Justice Holmes wrote that first amendment free speech rights do not extend to falsely shouting fire in a crowded theater. There are other examples. People can be thrown out of movie theaters for talking or from churches for screaming blasphemies. The character of the restrictions placed on free speech always depends on the character of the community doing the restricting and will vary according to whether we enter the community voluntarily or involuntarily (freedom of speech should probably be more carefully protected where there is no choice involved), according to its purpose (some monasteries allow no speech at all at certain times), according to its size (it is, for example, impossible for everyone to have his say in a group of even this size) and so on.

Now, if the purpose of college were solely to provide a comfortable and unthreatening place where young people could live together –

1 Originally part of a panel discussion on speech codes at Sarah Lawrence College in the fall of 1994.

that is, if it were a fraternity or sorority of sorts – it would not be so clear that it ought not place restrictions on what people say to each other. But it is also an academic community where the goal is finally not happiness or even comfort, but learning, and genuine learning requires, above all, an atmosphere in which one feels free to seek the truth because there are very few officially designated truths. The sort of questioning demanded by real education is frequently rather unsettling; it is not comfortable. When the two purposes of the institution are at odds in this way, it seems to me that the one ultimately providing its reason for being must prevail.

But even should we determine, as our present code does, that the possibility of having a decent community depends on the regulation of what can be said, determining what this means is hard, to say the least. New York State specifies two sorts of crimes under the category of harassment, first degree and second degree (Penal Code Sections 240.25 and 240.26). The two seem to differ primarily in terms of the seriousness of the threat involved. But they agree that harassment involves behavior that is intentional and repeated in such a way as to indicate a pattern. So they emphasize behavior rather than speech, although, of course, recognizing that insofar as speech frequently reveals the intent of action, it may be a kind of behavior. What they do not seem to cover is the sort of situation where someone says something once in anger that deeply offends someone else. They deal not so much with hurting people's feelings as with threats, verbal or not, to harm people physically.

The connection between this sort of behavior and speech is difficult to specify. If someone were to follow me around campus and in a menacing voice repeat over and over again "Davis," it certainly might annoy me to the point of being second degree harassment or under certain circumstances make me justifiably fear for my safety (first degree harassment). It would have little to do with what was said. On the other hand, let's take the word that perhaps most of all is by itself offensive – "nigger." It is even difficult to say it to use it as an example. Were you to use it in the heat of an argument, you should be blamed. It would indicate that you deserved to be held in contempt, but it need not mean that you were attempting to intimidate anyone. The word is a sign of prejudice, bad rearing, and lots of other things about the one who uses it, but by itself, it is not a sign of an intent to harm. It doesn't constitute harassment, and if it doesn't, I doubt that any word can be found that does.

I certainly do not mean to defend the use of deeply insulting language of this sort. The question is not whether it is decent behavior. The question is whether insults constitute behavior that should be regulated, whether any language should automatically be specified as harassment as for example in the following from our speech code: "The intentional use of offensive or insulting racial, gender, ethnic, religious, age, disability, or sexual orientation epithets, stereotypes, or characterizations to refer to or describe a person in that person's presence . . ."

Losing one's temper in a single verbal argument is not the same as a pattern of behavior intended as a threat. It may deserve contempt; it is not clear to me that it deserves probation, suspension, expulsion from the college, or any other official punishment. We need to remember that all bad things are not curable by passing regulations against them. Moral disapproval has a place in all communities.

Anyway, it is not clear that such rules will have much effect on prejudice. What is clear is that they set a precedent for outlawing certain words, and so set a precedent for outlawing certain thoughts – a dangerous precedent for an academic institution to set. We must try to make our college as decent a place as possible in which to live, but the underlying reason for the existence of the college has to be kept in mind. Threatening behavior has no place here, but we need to do our utmost to leave speech alone.

Chapter 4

LIBERAL EDUCATION AND LIFE[1]

I was initially reluctant to do this. Talking about education is a little like talking about a relationship – both are warning signs that there may not be anything to talk about. But I am here, so why don't I start by asking why this is so – i.e., what is it about education that makes it so hard to talk about (and, by the way, makes "school of education" almost an oxymoron)? One might say this. Education is only possible if there is something to learn – genuine knowledge of some kind. Otherwise education would simply be more or less sophisticated propaganda. What then is this stuff, knowledge?

Plato, whom it is always good to consult, wrote a dialogue called the *Theaetetus* in which the question "What is knowledge?" is raised. It divides roughly into two parts. In the first, Socrates' young interlocutor, Theaetetus, suggests an answer: perception. In the second, he suggests that knowledge is a kind of speech – true opinion.

Now, the thesis that knowledge is perception is attractive to us because it gives voice to our sense that knowledge must be confirmed by something outside of us – the real. Ironically, however, in the dialogue, Theaetetus gets his opinion that knowledge is perception from a book – Protagoras's *Truth*, the first line of which was "Man is the measure of all things, of the things that are, that they are, and of the things that are not, that they are not." So the thesis

1 Presented at Sarah Lawrence College, Fall 1997.

that knowledge is what we apprehend immediately ("seeing is believing") is mediated for Theaetetus through a book, and could only have been available in this way. For it might very well be the case that whatever we perceive is true, but if it were true it would be unsayable. Were everything simply what it seemed to be, how could I ever have any sense of what it means for something to seem? I would be immersed in a world that I could never have any cause to doubt. Talking, then, implies a certain distance or detachment or alienation from what is talked about.

On the other hand (this is the second part of the *Theaetetus*), the price of the distance from the world made possible by speech is that everything we say and understand can, by virtue of having been said, be repeated without understanding. This is a truth vividly apparent to anyone who has been around small children. Or think of a proof in geometry. The teacher works through the steps for you. You don't get it. She does it again, and again; she repeats it, say fifty times. You've got it by heart, but don't really know what you are saying. Suddenly something clicks. You say, "Aha! Now I've got it." The teacher says, "Show me," but all you can do is repeat the steps you have gone through now fifty-three times. What exactly is this "aha" then? It clearly doesn't consist in the steps – the speech or *logos*. Yet is it something one can have apart from the speech?

Knowledge seems, then, to be a combination of these two things – a speech or *logos* plus an immediate perception or intuition. Yet the "addition" of the perception is always invisible and will always elude speech. One of the jokes of Plato's *Theaetetus* is that the young Theaetetus and Socrates are said to be look-alikes – both very ugly. On the surface, then, it is not possible to distinguish one who does not know from one who presumably does. For Plato, this condition is central and ineradicable. There can be no surefire test to distinguish a philosopher from a sophist or genuine education from glibness.

Let's start again. In the parodos of Aeschylus's play *Agamemnon* the chorus utter a phrase usually taken to express the truth of Greek tragedy generally – *pathei mathos*, learning through suffering or experience (perhaps the two are the same). It is not enough to jump to the last page of *Oedipus the King* to see what happens to Oedipus. To learn, you have to undergo or experience the stages of what happens to him. This is why Aristotle names plot as the most important part of tragedy. The most extreme case of this view seems to be Aeschylus's Prometheus, who, as his name (Forethought) indicates, knew in advance exactly how he would be punished if he stole fire from heaven to give to mortals. We wonder how his fate can possibly be tragic; after all, he knew what he was getting into. Yet he did not, could not really know what it would feel like to be chained down and have his liver eaten daily by a bird. *Pathei mathos. . . .*[2] As Kant says in a different context, "Thoughts without content are empty; intuitions without content are blind."[3]

What does all of this give us? The distinguishing feature of real education seems not to admit of being formulated in speech. Accordingly, it is fair to say that no one ever got educated just by reading a list of books. In fact, many great books contain parodies of this sort of education. And many deeply educated people were not what we might call "culturally literate." Shakespeare may never have read Plato, and Plato certainly never read Shakespeare. At the same time, if the heart of education is unspeakable, education looks to be impossible, and, at the very least, you ought to begin to wonder about the $120,000 you are investing in it. What we have at our disposal is a tradition of "great works" – *logoi* or speeches. They are not great because they represent a list of approved answers; they are great because over time they have proven singularly powerful tools for inducing the sort of suffering or experience without which education is an empty shell. There are of course no guarantees, but if you read Plato's *Republic* for a semester, the odds are better that you will come to understand something of the question of justice – not simply in the sense that you will be given Plato's "view" of justice as one among a menu of possible choices, but rather that you will come to see what it is in the human soul that makes it inevitable that the question will be asked and then answered in a variety of

2 I am grateful to Seth Benardete for pointing this out to me.
3 Kant, Immanuel, *Kritik der Reinen Vernunft*, A 51. I have followed the Norman Kemp Smith translation.

inadequate ways. This is the plot of the *Republic* without which the theme is meaningless.

So what does all of this have to do with today's subject? Genuine education ought to maximize the chances that you will suffer the books you read, that you will not just acquire book-learning as though it were something you put in your pocket, but rather that you will treat learning as though your life depended on it – because it does.

Chapter 5

FIRST THINGS FIRST: HISTORY AND THE LIBERAL ARTS[1]

When Francis Randall[2] first approached me to give this talk we were standing on the path between Bates and Gilbert. He said – jokingly I thought at the time – that I ought to call the talk "First Things First." I laughed and said something that I have since forgotten. He did not forget, and here I am. I, of course, will disregard this history of my title and treat it instead as a text to be interpreted.

First things first – the phrase points to what is perhaps the most serious task for philosophy. Philosophy attempts to understand and reveal the underlying principles of all things. These principles are the first things partly in the sense in which we might talk about someone as the premier statesman of his "first" here meaning what is highest and best – but they are also first in the sense of most fundamental. They are notably not necessarily first temporally. It is not difficult to see that such principles, if they exist, are not self-evident. Were they self-evident, we would not have questions about our world; it would be immediately transparent. That we do have questions suggests to us that the things first in the sense of being most fundamental are not first in our experience. Or, as Aristotle puts it, there is a difference between what is first to us (donkeys, apples, dogs, lecture halls) and what is first by nature (substance, being, or

1 Presented at Sarah Lawrence College, Fall 1979.
2 Professor of History, Sarah Lawrence College.

perhaps god). Put somewhat differently, first things, alas, are not first. But if we cannot begin with what is truly first, where can we begin? It is in the context of this question that I would like to talk a little bit about history.

1. History and Poetry

In the *Poetics* Aristotle makes a famous comparison between poetry and history. Poetry, he says, is something more philosophic than history and of more importance. It is more important because it deals with what is universal whereas history deals with the particular. Two things startle our twentieth century ears here. First, we are, to say the least, unaccustomed to have something called important because it is more philosophic. Second, although we are quite fond of poetry, we are not necessarily fond of it because it has anything to do with universals. Rather, we admire it because it is the expression of the creativity of the individual or precisely because it deals so well with the particular. Poetry must be novel, and, of course, novels are in this sense poetic. These issues are related. We do recognize that philosophy deals with universals, but we have grave doubts about whether it accomplishes anything with them. It is one of the hallmarks of our age that to say that something is philosophic is frequently just shorthand for saying that it is merely philosophic, the latter, of course being a euphemism for its being irrelevant. Poetry, on the other hand, although it may have philosophic ambitions, need not. We are more comfortable with it because it does not seem so obviously Sisyphean. One of the more common obstacles to be overcome when students first come to study philosophy is their enthusiasm for the "fact" that it doesn't presume to give any answers.

Let us for the moment resist the temptation to believe what it is comfortable for us to believe and try to see what Aristotle had in mind. Poetry is not tied to what actually happens in the way history is tied. If in the course of this lecture a fire alarm goes off, and we are all forced to evacuate the building for three-quarters of an hour, something of the continuity of the lecture would be lost. This might be unfortunate, but it would not be particularly significant. However, if the same thing were to happen in a novel by Saul Bellow, the incident would be intended. I am reminded of the main character in Bellow's *Seize the Day*. He invests his last dollar in the commodities market – in lard. Why lard? This is the sort of question we are allowed, even invited to ask of *Seize the Day*. But if I were to invest my last dollar in lard, would the same apply? Nietzsche put all of this very well: "We know the subjective artist only as the bad artist."[3] For your art to have anything to say to me, you must appeal to something that we in some way at least potentially share in common.

Aristotle means, then, that the poet attempts to give things a significance that they in reality do not always have. Even those who wish to teach us about the power that chance has in our lives must endow the details of their poems with more than chance significance. It is by abstracting from the power of chance or happenstance in our lives that the poets can use the particular as a sign of something more than particular. The story of Oedipus is not simply the tale of one man's misfortunes; it is meant to show us something of the human condition. Now, history certainly can and does teach us about ourselves, but insofar as it seeks to be a representation of the way things were, it is necessarily bound up with what is accidental – what was but need not have been. For Aristotle, knowledge can never be of what is accidental, of what happened to happen.

2. History as a Paradigm for Knowledge

Supposing, then, that Aristotle is correct, i.e., that poetry and by implication philosophy have more cognitive dignity than history, that the knowledge they seek is concerned with the necessary connections among things, of what is always the same – put bluntly, supposing that history is not knowledge properly understood at all – supposing all of this, why is history the paradigm for us of what it means to know something? That this is so seems clear. A quick glance at the Sarah Lawrence College Catalogue, after you have gotten past the initial chaos of the course offerings, is revealing. While disciplines – dance, for example – may have ways of dividing themselves on the basis of their subject matters, the single method of division cutting across the boundaries of the various disciplines is

3   Friedrich Nietzsche, *The Birth of Tragedy*, section 5.

history (indeed, a second glance reveals that even dance has a category called *modern* dance). All of this is particularly important at an institution without traditional departments that encourages students to cut across boundaries. We study art, philosophy, politics, health care, music, dance, mathematics, science, and even ceramics with a view to their histories, although, of course, not exclusively. Still, it is not hard to see where you might turn to begin thinking the various parts of your education together. What is especially startling about all of this is that the classic texts in education – Plato's *Republic* is the most notable – are silent about history as a part of education. The history of this radical change in our understanding of education is of extraordinary interest. Its result is pretty clear. For us, to explain something means to place it within a history and give its history. Were I to ask any of you to tell me about yourselves, I suspect you would think that I must mean for you to relate your personal history. And I think that it is no accident that what many take to be the deepest thing to be said about a human being is all bound up with the sort of personal history that emerges in Freudian analysis.

When we begin to put some of these issues together, the following problem emerges:

History deals with what is accidental.
Knowledge deals with what is essential.
Yet, history is the paradigm for knowledge.

How do we reconcile these claims? Historically there are two sorts of ways out of this difficulty. On the one hand, we may deny that history deals with what is accidental. This means, of course, that what happens does not simply happen to happen. It is in some way necessary. The two most famous proponents of such a view are Marx and Hegel. One can describe the direction taken by Marx very crudely in the following way (as I am not sure one can describe Hegel's way crudely, I won't try). For Marx, what happens in history happens necessarily. The French Revolution is not something that might or might not have occurred; it is not in this sense accidental or contingent. Its necessity and the necessity of all the various events of history are rooted in the struggle among classes. The last of these struggles, as you probably well know, is between bourgeois and proletarian. The struggles themselves are necessary given certain predictable variations in the manner in which human beings produce things and so in the manner in which they are related to the things they produce. It is all enormously complicated and deserves careful study and consideration, but even from this caricature, you can begin to see several things. Marx denies that history is accidental and therewith denies the power of chance in history. On the one hand, this is clearly opposed to Aristotle's understanding of history. On the other hand, by endowing historical events with more than apparent significance, in a strange way Marx turns history into a poem. Like Tommy Wilhelm's dabbling in lard on the commodities market, historical events may appear accidental, but in the end they turn out to be significant. In denying Aristotle's view of history, Marx confirms Aristotle's view of knowledge. Put differently, since for Marx history is no longer accidental, it must have a structure, and this structure is itself transhistorical.

There is a second way to understand how history can emerge as a paradigm for what it means to know. We may deny the second of Aristotle's two premises – that knowledge deals with what is essential. This amounts to saying that we can never know anything but the particular. But what does this mean? On the most generous interpretation, it seems to mean that we can never do anything but record the passing of independent and unrelatable events. The events are unrelatable because to relate them would be to compare them, and to compare them suggests that they have something in common. That we can never know anything but the particular seems harmless enough until we realize that it rules out, for example, any attempt to compare two wars. Even to call them both wars is to have erred, for it means that we have already categorized and so generalized and accordingly are already well beyond the particular. To claim that knowledge does not deal with the essential is finally tantamount to denying that it is possible to know anything at all.

This second alternative is for us dominant. The flight to the particular that is so characteristic of our age is rooted in a deep-seated, although frequently concealed, pessimism. We are on the one hand convinced that the most important questions are not such as admit of answers. In our self-styled sophistication, we think it naïve to hope for answers to the questions of the best human life or the best political regime or the nature of the beautiful or the true. We are finally convinced that a final resolution of every issue of any importance to us is closed off to us. Yet we cannot leave it at that. The questions are too obviously important. We somehow cannot stop asking them. By making history the paradigm of what it means to know, we conceal from ourselves the fact that we do not think the most important things are really knowable. We are allowed to continue to ask the questions without expecting to get any answers.

3. History and Education

I think that it is fair to say that this pessimism is probably not the most advisable view to adopt at the outset of your education. The minimum that I would demand if I were you is that a view that is so destructive of the possibility of education should prove itself in competition with other views. I suppose I am urging you to take Aristotle seriously, and that, of course, means not taking history for granted. Remember that there was an age for which history did not have the same power as it has for us. There are also some things I do not want to leave you with the impression that I have said. For example, none of this means that history is useless, that you should not study history, that professors of history are unphilosophic, or that you should study philosophy. Our word *history* derives from the Greek *historia*, which means *inquiry*. History is the sort of inquiry that is invaluable both for theoretical reasons – i.e., because it will help you to learn about things that are worth knowing for their own sakes – and for practical reasons – i.e., because it will help you to get along better in the world. To say that history ought not be the paradigm for what it means to know means, rather, that the past is not necessarily important simply because it is past. A tradition is not valuable simply because it is tradition; it is rather a tradition because it has proven valuable. The study of history for its own sake can easily become a sort of antiquarianism and is cognitively indistinguishable from gossip. Perhaps this ought to cause us to revise our opinion of gossip as well as our opinion of history. Gossip contains many interesting things. When we envy the good fortune of another, that is, when we say, "So and so did not really deserve such and such," the other side of our envy is an implicit judgment about who deserves what in the world. The other side of envy is justice, and that is interesting.

Finally, you will have noticed that I have more than once inserted remarks about history – and apparently critical of history – that are themselves of an historical character. Why have I done that? In giving an historical account of our notion of history, one shows what happened but what perhaps need not have happened. Studying the contingent, the particular, the accidental, what happens by chance is one way to begin to understand the difference between the accidental and the necessary. Put simply, history does not deal with what is first by nature or essentially first; but it does deal with what is first for us. In doing so it provides us with what is perhaps the indispensable access to what is truly first.

Chapter 6

PHILOSOPHY IN THE COMICS[1]

I must begin with some confessions. I do read the *New York Times* – I am after all a college professor – but I have to admit to a certain thrill when the paper girl comes in the evening with the *White Plains Reporter Dispatch*.[2] We get it, of course, because it is very important to stay abreast of local issues. Well, actually, the first thing any of us do is turn to the comics. I will never forget the look of bewilderment on my daughter's face – she was about four – when she asked for the comics in the morning, and I told her that the *Times* had none. My second confession is that I am one of those people who first flips through the pages of the *New Yorker* for the cartoons and never returns for anything else. So, I start with a puzzle: why do these things have such power over a person otherwise obviously quite serious? I don't mean political cartoons, although I quite like them. Nor do I mean only "approved" cult strips like *Peanuts*, *Doonesberry*, and *The Far Side*. I mean *Beetle Bailey, Blondie, Rose is Rose*, and *Luann*, and, what is without question my favorite, *Calvin and Hobbes*. That someone had the chutzpah to name a comic strip after a philosopher and a theologian who, when taken together, may be said to have provided the foundation for America,

1 Presented in the Spring of 1989 at the Sarah Lawrence College Alumnae/i College.
2 Actually I must now confess that I no longer read the *New York Times*. Also, the White Plains paper is now called the *Journal News*.

is the best excuse I can think of for what I am about to do today. I want to try to understand the curious power of the funnies with the help – this is not a joke – of Aristotle. Now, this will involve doing what one is never supposed to do – explaining jokes. So forgive me in advance.

Let's look first at an example from Gary Larson's *The Far Side*.[3] Two policemen stand next to a tree in the middle of a forest. One holds a pillow in one hand and a bloodhound on a leash in the other. Leaning against a tree is a very tired looking goose plucked of all but a few feathers. The first policeman says to the dog, "You idiot! We want the scent on the pillow! *On* the pillow!"

What is the joke here? The police are presumably looking for a criminal. They have a pillow with his scent on it and want to use a bloodhound to follow the scent. But, instead, the dog follows the scent of the goose whose feathers were plucked to form the pillow. Why is this funny? Well, for one thing, it catches you having the same expectations as the policemen. And it shows you how silly you are to take those presuppositions for granted. In fact, the bloodhound is not so dumb. What the relevant scent is depends altogether on your interpretation of the prior situation.

A second *Far Side* cartoon provides another version of the same problem.[4] A man is asleep on a cot in a tent. A very large snake has slithered under the cot and lifted its head up to the the sleeping man. Its tongue touches the man's head. In the dream bubble above his head we see the man being caressed by a woman and saying "I love the way you do that, Angela... Oh, yes, yes, <u>yes</u>!" This is a spoof of Freud; it amounts to asking why snakes have to be symbols for sex. Why can't sex be a symbol for snakes?

But let us return to the first cartoon; its particulars are instructive. What is at stake is the status of the pillow. From the point of view of the policemen, the pillow is the thing and the feathers are just the matter that makes up the thing. For the dog, however, the *feathers* are the thing. The police and the dog thus give two dis-

---

3 For the cartoon image see Larson, Gary *The Far Side Gallery 3* (Kansas City and New York: Andrews and MacMeel, 1984), p. 121.
4 For the image see *The Far Side Gallery 3*, p. 131.

crepant answers to the question, What is this thing before me? The difference turns on what Aristotle would have called the material cause of the object. In the first book of his *Metaphysics* and the second book of his *Physics*, Aristotle spells out four possible answers to the question, What is *x*? One can answer by identifying the matter or underlying stuff (*hupokeimenon*) from which something is made. The statue *is* bronze, the pillow *is* feathers. One can say the statue is a horse and thereby identify its being with its form or looks (*eidos*). One can identify the statue with the immediate cause of its coming to be formed or shaped as it is, for example, pouring the bronze of the statue into a mold. This is the efficient cause or cause of motion. Finally, one can answer the question, What is it? with the end or purpose for the sake of which the being came to be – what Aristotle calls the final cause. The statue could *be* a monument to a famous horse. What Larsen's cartoon calls attention to is that answers to these questions are not simply separable from one another. What something is made of is not so obvious as it seems. True, the pillow is made of feathers and the statue of bronze, but as soon as you turn your "what is" question on the underlying stuff your answer will give *it* a form and, therefore, necessarily assume some *formed* stuff underlying it. Bronze is a form or kind of metal, and feathers are a kind of animal tissue. The dog appears to be at a deeper level of inquiry than the police.

We could, of course, go deeper still. Ultimately, to say what something is in terms of its matter, we would have to think in terms of some prime matter, out of which all else is formed. But what could be said of such matter? To say what something is means to give it a form – that is, to speak about something always must mean to speak about a kind of thing. The man said to have been the first philosopher, Thales, was said to have made the claim that the stuff out of which all else is made is water. And yet, if everything is water why does everything not have the characteristics of water? If everything is water, why isn't everything wet? Or, to be more precise, if everything is water how can anything be wet? The underlying stuff of which *everything* consists cannot be said to have the attributes of anything in particular. It is indistinguishable from nothing. The question, What is *x*? therefore finally pushes us back to stuff that is inarticulable. The attempt to say what something is simply by saying what it is made of thus proves impossible. Accordingly, underneath Larsen's cartoon is an insight into what makes a reductionist, materialist account of the world impossible.

Let us turn briefly to two more examples. The first is by Stan Hunt and from the *New Yorker*.

"Morrison, you know, has always had extremely sound judgment, but he has never had occasion to exercise it."

From The New Yorker Collection. Reprinted with permission.

The joke here is that judgment is the sort of thing one can have only by exercising it.[5] Once again, there is a parallel in Aristotle. In the first and then again in the second book of the *Nicomachean Ethics*, Aristotle points to how difficult it is to define virtue. It

---

5 The tendency to think otherwise recalls the famous first sentence of Descartes's *Discourse on Method*: "Good sense is the best distributed thing in the world because each thinks himself to be so well provided with it that even those who are most difficult to please in every other thing are not at all accustomed to desire more of it than they have."

cannot simply be a potentiality, for there has to be something actual or real about it. On one level, just by being alive we are potentially courageous or wise. And even if we have a propensity toward courageous acts or wise thoughts, we are not virtuous if we never exercise that propensity. We do not call babies virtuous, nor would we say that someone who slept his whole life was virtuous. Yet virtue is not simply the same as the virtuous action. We all know that it is possible to do good things without being good. In fact, this is how we teach children to be virtuous. If it is anything, then, virtue must somehow be a cross between pure potentiality – i.e., possibility – and actuality. Aristotle calls this mixture a *hexis*, a disposition or, literally, a having (the verb, *echô*, from which *hexis* derives means either "to have" or "to be able.") What we call character is clearly something of this sort – an actualized potentiality. This cartoon points to this strange character of virtue by pointing to half of the problem – i.e., unexercised good judgment is ridiculous.

The next example, a Luann strip by Greg Evans, describes me in 1960 and my daughter thirty years later.

Reprinted with the permission of United Media.

Things changed a lot during those years, especially with regard to sex, but apparently something remained constant. Still, that something is a "timeless truth" ought not be enough to make it funny. So what is funny here? Isn't it that those whose sole desire is to be together should express this desire by being totally apart? Consider Aristotle's criticism of Plato's *Republic* in the second book of his *Politics*.

> For we think friendship to be the greatest of goods for the city (since in this way it would have the least internal strife). And Socrates especially praises the city for being one, which seems

to be and he says to be the work of friendship, just as in his erotic speeches we know that Aristophanes speaks of lovers as being such great friends that they desire to grow together and both come to be one from being two. But here it is necessary that both or one have perished. . . . (1262b8–14)

This difficulty is perhaps felt most powerfully by adolescents. Longing to be together requires separation. Love is a longing to be together (the Greek *sunousia* means literally being together but really either sexual intercourse or a lecture) that can only be experienced when we are apart. At an eighth grade dance you are defining yourself, individuating yourself, separating yourself in terms of your longings – your *eros*. This experience consists in feeling apart from the object of longing. Were this gap to close it would be necessary that "both or one have perished."

What does this series of examples add up to? It is not exactly a scientific sample; still, let's say that cartoons or comics seem particularly fertile places for philosophical questioning. To see why this might be the case it is helpful to turn once again to Aristotle.

For on account of wondering, men both now and at first began to philosophize, wondering from the beginning about the perplexities (*aporiai*) close at hand, and then, moving forward by small steps, also being perplexed by the greater, such as about what the moon undergoes, and the sun and the stars, and about the coming to be of everything. But one who is perplexed and wonders considers himself ignorant (hence also the lover of myth [*philomuthos*] is somehow a lover of wisdom [*philosophos*]; for a myth is composed of wonders). So that if they philosophized to flee ignorance, it is clear that they pursued science [*to epistasthai*] to know [*to eidenai*] and not for the sake of some use. The events themselves bear witness to this, for such wisdom [*phronêsis*] began to be sought for recreation and to pass the time, when almost all necessities were provided for. It is clear then that we seek it for the purpose of no use other than itself, but just as we say a free man is for the sake of himself and not another, so also this alone of the sciences [*epistêmôn*] is free. For it itself alone is for the sake of itself. (*Metaphysics*, 982b11–28)

Its acquisition, however, must somehow result in the opposite of the beginning of our inquiries. For everyone begins, as we said, from wondering whether it holds thus, as [they do] about the self-movement of puppets or about the solstices and equinoxes or the incommensurability of the diagonal [of the square with its sides]. For it seems wondrous to all of those not yet having seen the cause if something is not measurable by its least dimension. But it must end at the opposite and, according to the proverb, better state, as [holds] even in those cases when they learn. For the geometrical man would wonder at nothing so much as if the diagonal should become measurable. (*Metaphysics*, 983a11–24)

That philosophy *always* begins in wonder means that it is not progressive; it does not allow for building on the work of previous generations. Rather, if the beginning is always the same, the initial perplexities at which we wonder must still be with us. What Aristotle does not mean is what he had begun the whole *Metaphysics* with, namely, that "all men by nature desire to know." This could simply amount to a desire to replace a perceived ignorance by knowledge. You do not know how to get to the Bronxville train station; so you ask. Or, you do not know what someone has been doing since graduation; so you write, or telephone, or go to a reunion. Wonder involves something else – another sort of awareness of not knowing, where what you do not know is on an altogether different plane from what you do know. Coming to know is, therefore, not simply an addition but, rather, a fundamental transformation of what you thought you knew. Ordinarily a desire to know is simply the attempt to transform something opaque into something plain. But wonder is the recognition that one does not know the cause of the ordinary and every-day. We come to see that the unhidden is really hidden.

This can be seen in a simple way. We are at first puzzled by eclipses. Why does the sun sometimes fail to shine? This ordinary perplexity in the face of the strange or wondrous leads us to inquire. In the course of our inquiry we discover that the reason why the sun is sometimes eclipsed is identical to the reason for its being most of the time not eclipsed. The cause of the unusual is, when properly understood, the same as the cause of the ordinary. Accordingly, a perceived irregularity of nature that causes us to wonder at what is strange ends by causing us to wonder that things are as they are ordinarily. We are moved to wonder that the sun moves as it does and not at why it sometimes diverges from this motion.

This sort of change of perspective is not easy. As there are not all that many eclipses to force our natural desire to know in this direction, philosophy requires an artificial nudge. Thus, when Aristotle says lovers of myth (*philomuthoi*) are "somehow" philosophers, he seems to mean that myths, stories, and tall tales are like artificial eclipses. Oedipus's strangeness – he kills his father and marries his mother – is meant to provide the impetus to wonder about what is most ordinary and likely to be taken for granted, mothers and fathers. The second chapter of *Genesis* tells us that human beings did not always labor and die and that women did not always give birth or feel the pains of labor so as to force us to reflect on the significance of these regularities of our natures. Now, this is something like what the funnies do. When we laugh, we bring to awareness what was hitherto hidden in the obvious. Cartoons and comics help us to wonder and so to be philosophic. This whole process is rather beautifully described in Norman MacLean's novella, *A River Runs Through It:*

> "All there is to thinking," he said, "is seeing something noticeable which makes you see something you weren't noticing which makes you see something that isn't even visible." (92)

But we should not end so seriously. The last example is a *Peanuts* strip by Charles Schulz.

Sally sees something essential about this activity we have been describing. It is so ordinary-looking from the outside as to look boring. At best it looks ridiculous. In looking afresh at the ordinary you seem not to see what everybody else sees on the must rudimentary level. Nothing is more disconcerting that to ask a question in class designed to show that the question *is* a question and have someone answer it. To begin to understand Sophocles's *Antigone*, one must let the question, Why bury dead bodies? hang ominously in the air. Some years ago in upstate New York, I came upon one of those temporary signs, a small trailer with an illuminated message: "Philosophy is just common sense in a dress suit." Now, this is in a way true; philosophy consists in reflecting on the obvious. But that it is dressed up means that it shows the common in such a way as to let its strangeness shine through. This is more difficult than it first appears, for the activity of thinking, really thinking, does not show itself. Think of movies about teaching and about how bad they ordinarily are. When teaching takes place, a teacher says something that makes rockets go off inside the students' minds. But as the whole point is that they *are* inside, any attempt to render them on the outside misrepresents their true nature. So instead we get Sidney Poitier making a salad in *To Sir With Love*. Philosophers are, therefore, not the stuff of which poetic (or television) heroes are fashioned. When they do make an appearance, they tend to look rather comical, like Socrates in Aristophanes's play, *The Clouds* or Thales falling into a well while gazing at the heavens to the amusement of a slave girl watching nearby. Of course, this should make us wonder. . .

Part Two

EXPERIENCE AND BOOKS

Chapter 7

THE ONE BOOK COURSE: AN INTERNSHIP IN THE IVORY TOWER[1]

My original plan was to entitle this talk "Learning Book Learning: An Internship in the Ivory Tower." My old friend Bradd Shore, who brought me here today, forbade this title on the quite sensible grounds that it was unintelligible. Not knowing what on earth it was to be about, no one would come to hear the talk. He suggested "The One Book Course." I countered with "The One Book Course: An Internship in the Ivory Tower," reversing standard academic practice so that the post-colon (post-colonial?) explanatory subtitle is even more obscure than the main title. Now Bradd is clearly right that one cannot be interested in what is altogether opaque. To find something interesting – to think that it is in our interest to attend to it – we must know what we are getting into. And yet, were we unable to be interested in what we do not know, we could never learn anything. It would be a strange education, and I think not a particularly lively one, that consisted in learning only what we already knew. So apparently we find interesting only what is at once known and unknown, transparent and opaque. This is the very structure of asking a question – to specify and so know what

1 Originally delivered as a lecture to the Anthropology Department at Emory University in April 2000.

we do not know. Accordingly, to teach is to attract students on the basis of what they know so as to reveal to them what they do not know. The name of this venerable educational principle is "bait and switch." I will follow it today in an attempt to show Bradd Shore what I had in mind by the first title. That I get to do this in a gathering of this kind has the added advantage that I am allowed to talk until I am finished, and Bradd must at least feign listening.

For about twenty-five years now I have been offering semester-long courses on single texts – Plato's *Republic,* but also his much shorter *Laches, Lysis,* and *Symposium*; Aristotle's *Politics, Nicomachean Ethics,* and *Metaphysics,* but again also his short book the *Poetics*; Descartes's *Discourse on Method* and *Passions of the Soul*; Rousseau's *Emile, Reveries,* and *Of the Social Contract*; Nietzsche's *Thus Spoke Zarathustra* and *Genealogy of Morals*; Heidegger's *Being and Time.* These are a fairly representative sample of the texts I have read one at a time with students at both the undergraduate and graduate levels. I have been tempted by Greek tragedy but hesitant to try with students who do not have the language. The closest I've got was a two book course – Plato's *Hippias Major* and Euripides' *Helen* (but more on that later). I certainly make no claim to be particularly innovative; from my undergraduate years on, this is how I learned from the best of my teachers. They, in turn, were similarly taught by their teachers, most of whom were part of that generation of émigré-scholars educated in German universities, where one book seminars still remain fairly common.

Now it is clear that there are a number of assumptions involved in deciding to teach in this way. The book to be read has to be pretty good if it is to warrant an entire semester. Still, such books are not as rare as we are wont to think. It has always seemed to me strange that we should expect to spend so much less time understanding a book than it took its author to think it – strange, for example, that Dante should devote twenty years to so artfully constructing the *Divine Comedy* while we have the expectation of "getting it" in two weeks just before we move on to Boccacio, not to mention the *hybris* of breezing through Tolstoy's *War and Peace* in a week or so when its title announces that its theme will be, well . . . everything. And then, of course, if we are to spend an entire term on one book, the book will either have to be very long indeed or we will have to read excruciatingly slowly. Nietzsche has a remark *a propos* of this:

> In order to practice reading as an art . . . one thing is necessary above all, what nowadays has come to be so well unlearned – and for that reason there is still time until my writings are "readable" – for which one must be nearly a cow and in any case not a "modern human being": *rumination.*[2]

At the very least "rumination" means rereading with the assumption that our first impressions were only that and did not take us to the heart of the matter. There are a variety of possible causes for our superficiality. Authors may intentionally seduce us into an initial misreading; that is, they may make our very tendency to misunderstand them and to bring unwarranted assumptions to their texts a part of what they wish to teach us – this, I think, is the case with Plato and with the Greek tragedians. Or they may see that, as one cannot do everything at once, one must start by treating something as simply true that will emerge as true in only a qualified way after the argument is further developed – in different ways this is true of both Aristotle and Heidegger. Or they may try to give us everything at once and for this very reason present us with a surface that is enormously complex and needs to be continually rethought – this I think (although less confidently) is the case with Kant and Hegel. One therefore need not believe in the widespread practice of esoteric writing (although I do) to see why it is worthwhile to spend a great deal of time on one book. But the minimal conditions *are* first that one believe that the world is hard – it needs interpretation – and second that chewing the cud is not mere self-indulgence, but brings with it the reward of an increasingly deepening understanding. That is, not only does the world need interpreting; it also admits of interpreting. (The first assumption of a one-book course, then?) Because the world is hard, a work that really teaches us about it will perforce also be hard. The ancient Greeks had a proverbial saying: *khalepa ta kala* – "the beautiful things are hard." Hard things take time to

2 *On the Genealogy of Morals*, Preface, section 8 (the translation is my own).

digest. To understand the virtue of the one book course we would thus need an account of education as digestion – something like a digestive tract.

Close to the end of the *Republic*, in the tenth book, Plato has Socrates renew an attack on poetry begun in Books 2 and 3. This account of the "ancient quarrel [or difference] between poetry and philosophy" is not simply to be taken at face value. Book ten may begin with an attack on poetry; it nevertheless ends with a poem. The attack on poetry, as is well known, involves an attack on *mimêsis* – imitation. (Socrates will attack poetic imitation as giving us versions of things three steps removed from the truth – as if the poet goes around with a mirror simply reflecting objects he finds in the world; this alone should make us suspicious, since in the list of objects so reflected Socrates includes gods.) In the course of their inquiry into the nature of *mimêsis*, Socrates and his interlocutor, Glaucon, have the following conversation:

> Do you wish, then, [this is Socrates speaking] that we begin by inquiring from this point according to the customary procedure? For we are accustomed, I suppose, in the case of each particular many to set up one particular idea (*eidos*) by which we apply the same name. Or do you not understand?
>
> I understand.
>
> Then let us also now set up whichever many you wish. For example, if you want, there are, I suppose, many couches and tables.
>
> Surely.
>
> But there are indeed, I suppose, two ideas (*ideai*) of these implements, one of couch and the other of table.
>
> Yes.
>
> Therefore we are also accustomed to say that the craftsman of each of the implements, while looking toward the idea (*idea*) in this way the one makes the couches and the other the tables that we use, and other things in the same way. For, I suppose, none of the craftsmen crafts the idea (*idea*) itself. For how could he? (596a5–b10)

Now, the words *eidos* and *idea* are synonyms in Greek; both are cognate with the verb "to see," and both mean something like form. They are the "ideas" of the much heralded Platonic "theory of ideas." Here, however, Socrates seems to make an interesting, if rather arbitrary, distinction. When speaking of an idea or form as the unifying seal placed over a many when we know *that* the many is a one (for example, when we specify a variety of things with the single designation "table") but not *how* it is a one, he uses *eidos*. When talking about the form we look at in order to fashion copies of it, he uses *idea*. So in the present context, *eidos* stands for a dimly intuited object of inquiry – we must think we are looking for some one thing even to begin to search – while *idea* stands for something so fully known that by itself it can serve as a measure of and paradigm for other things – it is a sort of blue print.

In another famous passage of the *Republic* in Book 6, Socrates provides an image of the ways in which our various cognitive faculties are related. Dividing a line in sections, he assigns to each section a faculty of cognition and its appropriate object. Of this, one of the most celebrated and argued passages in Plato, I do not propose to try to give a full account. Suffice it to notice that in the course of developing his complicated image, Socrates describes two sorts of thinking: one that treats principles or beginning points (*archai*) as fixed and known and argues *from* them, and one that he calls dialectic which makes "hypotheses not *archai* [beginnings or first principles] but hypotheses in reality, i.e., means of access and springboards, for the sake of reaching the non-hypothetical at the beginning (*archê*) of the whole" (511b5–7). In other words, (Aristotle's words) thinking moves either *from* first principles or *to* first principles; the former movement presupposes that we already know what we are talking about, the latter that we do not yet know what we are talking about. A model for the one is the geometric proof; for the other, the one book course.

My course on Plato's *Hippias Major* and Euripides' *Helen* was entitled "The Drama of the Beautiful," reflecting my initial understanding of their common theme (their *idea*) – the question of beauty. Now, this turns out not to be altogether wrong, but neither is it altogether right. Halfway through *Helen*, I realized what I really thought the play was about – the nature of personal identity. What did it mean that not Helen but an identical phantom image, undetectable as an image even to her lover and husband, went to Troy and was the face that launched a thousand ships? Confronted, midway through the course, with good reasons to abandon the principle that had justified pairing the two works, I had to decide which it would be: a false but clear unity or a true and muddy discrepancy. What was true of this two-book course is true for every multi-book course, which, of necessity, moves *from* that first principle according to which it was originally planned in such a way as potentially to forestall a movement *to* another principle that is more genuinely first. A not uninteresting feature of standard academic jargon is that we speak of putting a course together. Courses put things together, they syn-thesize or even syl-logize. On the one hand this is enormously useful; on the other hand it can easily get in the way of learning.

I certainly do not want to condemn outright the practice of reading a lot of books in one course or teaching a variety of subjects with a prior view of how they all fit together. We are hired as teachers, after all, precisely because we are supposed to *know* something, and this is precisely the sort of thing we are supposed to know. We organize for our students a world of things – a universe of discourse – to be learned so that they can appropriate things more efficiently than were they to happen upon them just randomly. And what about the books I am advocating that we treat with such care and at such length? Aren't they too governed by a principle of selection? One could even go so far as to say that were the world *not* organized for us in terms of *ideai* – fixed beginning points (*archai*) – learning would be altogether impossible. Doesn't language perform this function by mediating between us and the world? Still, there is a peculiar virtue of reading one thing at a time. You begin with a book about which you have some hunches; you may even think you know what it is about. In any case, it is not a bad bet to think that something important is going on, say, in Plato's *Republic*. Maybe it is a description of the perfectly just political order – a politics perfectly compatible with idealism. Maybe it is a description of the impossibility of any perfectly just political order or a critique of politics in the name of a philosophical idealism. Maybe it is the most powerful critique of philosophical idealism ever written. You don't need to have settled these questions in order to teach the book. You don't even have to believe that in the end they will be the questions with which the book is most truly concerned. Once you have decided to read the *Republic* and have assumed that it means something, it becomes for you not an *idea* but an *eidos*. It presents itself as one and yet the principle of its oneness has not yet been determined. A course on a single book thus reproduces the experience of reading a book for the first time. We can see that everything is bound together between the two covers. We know *that* we are confronting something that is supposed to be a whole, but at the outset we do not yet know and cannot know *why*. To be sure, books can disappoint us; they can fail to hang together. But reading is the act of trying to make this not happen. We strive to make the plurality before us a whole, a one. The virtue of a one book course is thus that this characteristic of thinking, what Plato calls in *Republic* Book 6 dialectic, is necessarily brought to the fore. In studying a book, we learn about something in particular, say justice, in stages, progressively revising what we think to have settled; that is, we learn dialectically. But since dialectic is the heart of learning, one book courses are inevitably always also about learning – hence as a title "The One Book Course" is not so very far from "Learning Book Learning."

What about "An Internship in the Ivory Tower?" Aren't these two notions quite at odds? That is, are not internships meant to get students out of the ivory tower, to get their hands dirty in the experience of life as it is really lived apart from the various idealisms of the academy? I wonder why we so quickly assume that it is easy for students to "get" what is going on in the academy, while at the same time assuming it is so hard for them to get what goes on in the "real" world. While this understanding of reality seems to me to be rather too taken for granted, there is still something revealing about the attractiveness of internships.

The earliest articulation of the principle of internships known to me occurred in 558 b.c., the year of the first performance of Aeschylus's tragic trilogy, the *Oresteia*. In the parados of Aeschylus's *Agamemnon* (177), a chorus of men already too old to go to war ten years ago describe the events leading up to the sacrifice of Iphigeneia by Agamemnon that allowed the Greeks to sail to Troy. The principle they articulate, *pathei mathos* – learning through suffering, experiencing, or undergoing is frequently understood to be the principle of tragic wisdom generally; its context here is particularly interesting. We have no idea how the chorus know the details of the sacrifice of Iphigeneia until they tell us that they averted their eyes at the last minute just before Agamemnon cut Iphigeneia's throat. So we learn belatedly that these old men were there at Aulis, some eighty miles as the crow flies (and as old men seldom fly) from their home in Argos. Why? Weren't they too old to go to war with Agamemnon? Well, clearly someone had to bring Iphigeneia to Aulis so that Agamemnon could sacrifice her; presumably he did not bring her along at the outset on the off-chance that he might need a daughter to sacrifice. Since all the able-bodied men were already with the army, who but those represented by the chorus were available as an escort? So, in fact, this chorus, who present themselves as pure observers and reporters, are in this whole sordid affair of human sacrifice up to their necks. It is a deep irony that immediately after they unwittingly give us the evidence of their guilt, they rearticulate their principle of human wisdom – "Justice allots learning to those who suffer" (250). That one learns by suffering casts a certain doubt on the objectivity of what is learned. And, like the chorus of the *Agamemnon*, we have come to the plot in a way that is not altogether neutral. We know of the sacrifice of Iphigeneia, and at the beginning of the play we tend to side with the chorus. Yet, if we have been paying attention, our initial impression must change with the addition of this new piece to the puzzle – they were at Aulis. We too have learned by suffering.[3]

3   For this interpretation of the chorus, see Seth Benardete's "On Greek Tragedy" in *The Argument of the Action: Essays on Greek Poetry and Philosophy* (Chicago: 2000), 122.

From the Greek verb for suffering, *paskhô*, comes *pathos* (both theirs and ours) and ultimately "passion" – meaning, on the one hand emotion, and, on the other, what is opposed to action. The passivity of passion is connected to the fact that experiencing the world means running up against things for which we are not responsible, things that we cannot change. To experience means to hit resistance. It is only a small step from this to the notion that to undergo passively is to suffer or be pained. Something similar occurs with our word "self-conscious," which means being aware of oneself in an altogether neutral sense but also means what seventh-grade boys once felt (and perhaps still feel) at junior high school dances.

Now, to say that we learn through suffering but that our suffering skews what we think we have learned is another way of describing the fact that all learning begins with what we sort of know but do not really know. Learning invariably begins in error. This is perhaps most obvious when we realize that in learning it is never possible for us at the outset to know what we are doing. If we did, we would already know where we were headed. Even a deductive proof requires a hunch about the conclusion. Without anticipating what we wanted to prove, we would have no way to know when we were done with the proof. And, as the form of a deduction requires that each step be fully justified on the basis of what has come before, *any* step could be the end of the proof. Many years ago, Bradd Shore and I organized a lecture series together – an intramural series at the small college where we both taught. We were new at our jobs and thought it a good way to get to know colleagues in the faculty at large. One of the people we asked to speak was an aging sociologist – I won't name him – who, I hope, had seen better days. He gave a long rambling talk, impossible to follow, darting from one thing to another without any apparent connection. An hour into the talk, I whispered to Bradd, who was sitting next to me, "How will we know when he's done?" to which Bradd responded "How will *he* know when he's done?" Without the anticipation of an end, thinking is aimless – not really thinking – and deduction becomes indistinguishable from rambling. However, the anticipation of an end must come before the end, and this means that it comes before we have any right to it.

Accordingly, we must always begin without knowing whether we begin correctly. This open-endedness is a necessary feature of learning. The first line of the *Iliad* is "Sing goddess of the anger of Peleus's son, Achilles." To understand the sentence presumably one must know what Homer means by anger. Yet it is not unreasonable to think that just this, anger, is the theme of the *Iliad*, which as a whole is meant to form our understanding of its causes, consequences, and nature. Accordingly, one cannot *really* understand the first line until one has understood the poem as a whole. If we really learn from the *Iliad*, then, our first understanding of anger must have been only partial, and so flawed. It is our fate always to be in over our heads.

Aeschylus's *Prometheus Bound* provides a particularly stark example of this principle.[4] It seems almost a test case for tragedy, which ordinarily involves a character's discovery or recognition of the unforeseen consequences of his actions. But Prometheus, the Titan whose very name means forethought, knew exactly what would happen to him if he stole fire from heaven to give to men. His punishment is severe – having your liver eaten by an eagle each day is a peculiarly unpleasant version of the eternal return of the same – but it cannot have been unanticipated by the man who introduces himself by saying,

> All that is to come to be I know accurately in advance; nor shall
> any calamity come to me unexpected. (101–3)

How then can the story of Prometheus's fate be a tragedy? Prometheus may know *that* his liver will be eaten each day, but can he really know how this will feel until it happens, until he suffers it? To be able to *say* what will happen is thus not really to *know* what will happen, for if knowledge amounted to being able to provide true speeches, everyone who could mouth the words would be wise, and wisdom would be indistinguishable from a good memory.[5]

In the *Prometheus*, Aeschylus shows us how deeply human knowledge depends on experience – *pathei mathos*. Plato's version of this problem is the dialogue, *Theaetetus*, in which the doubleness

---

4   See pages 26–27 above.
5   I owe this insight to Seth Benardete.

of knowledge is presented as the problematic combination of perception and an account, a *logos*.[6] The first does justice to our sense that our knowledge is confirmed by the immediate presence of what is apart from us. The second does justice to our sense that to apprehend what is other than us we must be apart from it – alienated; knowledge can only come to us mediately through *logos*. This alienation *from* is rather nicely symbolized by the book.

Knowledge combines two things – a speech or *logos* plus an immediate perception or intuition – suffering, but it is not so clear what it would mean to know this combination. Can we have knowledge of knowledge? No speech could ever capture the experience that must be "added" to speech if it is not simply to be rote learning. Imagine Prometheus's description of his fate before he suffers it. Now imagine a second description after he has suffered it. How would the two differ? Not only are the young Theaetetus and Socrates ugly look-alikes; accompanying Theaetetus at the outset of the dialogue is one of his contemporaries, a young man named Socrates. How are we to distinguish Socrates from his look-alike when we see them or from his name-sake when we hear of them? On the surface, then, neither by perception nor by speech is it in principle possible to distinguish one who presumably does know from those who do not. There can be no formula for distinguishing a philosopher from a sophist because there is no acid test of genuine learning.

Courses in which the received wisdom on a subject is simply presented in its finished form always run the risk of transmitting the words but not the music – that is, without the pathos of knowledge. Strictly speaking there is no solution to this problem; such misunderstanding is a possibility coeval with speech. Non-strictly speaking, however, a course in which one book is read with great care, and with the expectation that one's first and even subsequent impressions will necessarily be provisional and so meant to be repeatedly replaced by later, fuller, deeper understandings, can provide experience in the sort of thinking-through of problems that underlies the greatest books. Reading of this sort is not just book learning; it is

6 See pages 25–26 above.

training in the sequence of enchantment and disenchantment and re-enchantment that must characterize the process of learning. In suffering the great books, we learn what it means to learn by suffering and so are provided not simply with a doctrine to carry away in our pockets, but with experience in the everyday practice of the theoretical life – an internship in the Ivory Tower.

So far all of this has been strangely abstract, as a general account of the benefit of immersing oneself in a particular book unfortunately must be. If the proof of the pudding is in the eating (*pathei mathos*), what I have given so far amounts at the very best to some preliminary inducements to taste the pudding. Let me supplement this with some examples – some rather extended, some less so – of the sort of chewing I have in mind.

Let us turn, after a little background, to the very first words of Sophocles' *Oedipus Tyrannus*.[7] Much of the action necessary for understanding the play occurs before it even opens. Everything begins with the oracle received by Laius, king of Thebes, saying that his son will kill him (720–22) and perhaps his wife, Jocasta, as well (1176). Accordingly, when Oedipus is born, his father pierces the baby's feet and gives him to a servant to abandon on Mt. Cithaeron near Thebes (717–19). Jocasta never expresses any remorse over this even after indicating that she has grave doubts about the reliability of oracles (707–9). The servant disobeys and hands Oedipus over to a herdsman – a servant to Polybus, King of Corinth. This herdsman gives Oedipus to Polybus and his wife, Merope, who raise him as their son. Now, after Oedipus grows up he overhears a drunk say that he is not the son of Polybus and Merope. He confronts his parents with this charge, which they deny, but Oedipus, still suspicious, travels to Delphi to consult the oracle of Apollo. Instead of an answer to his question, he receives oracle number two: that he will kill his father and have intercourse with his mother. Horrified at this prospect, Oedipus flees from Corinth. Apparently he believes in o

---

7   Much of the following interpretation is greatly indebted to two extraordinary articles by Seth Benardete – "Sophocles' *Oedipus Tyrannus*" in *Ancients and Moderns*, Joseph Cropsey, ed. (New York: Basic Books, 1964), 1–15 and "On Greek Tragedy," in *Current Developments in the Arts and Sciences, The Great Ideas Today 1980* (Chicago: *Encyclopaedia Britannica*, 1980), 102–43.

racles enough to run away but not enough to believe that what they foretell will necessarily come to pass – and, of course, he wants to avoid becoming a subject for Freud. Now, on the way from Delphi to Thebes Oedipus comes upon a party of travelers – there seem to have been five (752). The Herald tells him to get out of the way, but Oedipus will not. At this point the leader of the party, the one riding in a cart, hits Oedipus on the head with his goad. Oedipus proceeds to kill the whole group (perhaps this is a little excessive for a traffic dispute), which seems to be Laius and his entourage on the way to Delphi to consult the oracle – we are not told why. Meanwhile, back at Thebes, after Laius leaves but before Oedipus arrives, a monster (a sphinx – part woman and part lion) is exacting a flesh and blood tribute until someone solves her riddle: What walks on four legs in the morning, two at midday, and three in the evening? Oedipus arrives, solves the riddle (the answer is man – first in infancy, then in his prime, and finally in old age), gets the kingship and Jocasta as his wife for a reward, and serves the Thebans well for what seems to be fifteen to twenty years. He and Jocasta have two daughters and an unspecified number of sons. At this point there is a new plague; no birth of any kind – plant or animal – occurs in Thebes, nor any burial. Oedipus sends his brother-in-law, Creon, to Delphi to ask the oracle what to do (it turns out that the cause of the plague is that Laius's murderer is still at large), and, on Creon's advice, also sends for the seer, Teiresias. This is where the play opens. All of this information is given to us retrospectively as the play proceeds.

Given its complexities, to say that the plot thickens would certainly be an understatement. Sophocles himself points to the first problem and, by doing so, provides a model for how to read him. Oedipus says that he killed all of those he met on the road (813), but in fact one of the servants of Laius survived (118). This servant reports that the party was set upon by robbers, that the deed could not have been done by one man (122–23). Although Oedipus at first ignores this inconsistency and asks how the robber could have dared this deed (124), eventually he notices it and, concluding that "a one could not be equal to many" (845), he sends for the servant to resolve the discrepancy. By the time the servant arrives (1110 ff.), however, the incest issue has so overwhelmed Oedipus that he doesn't even ask the question that might clear him of the murder of his father. This is particularly puzzling since it is this unresolved murder that is supposed to be causing the plague. Now, it might strain the suspension of disbelief to accept the coincidence of two killings at the same crossroads in one day, but is it any more difficult than the various other "Gilbert and Sullivan" coincidences in the play – for example, the fact that the servant sent from Corinth to announce the death of Polybus should be the very herdsman to whom the baby Oedipus was entrusted. What is crucial is that by assuming his guilt concerning what is for Thebes *the* most important issue, Oedipus jumps the gun. He acts as though he knows when he does not know – and so do we.

There are several other problems in the plot. We are supposed to believe that although Oedipus knew Laius had died (105), he has lived at least fifteen years in Thebes, and no one has mentioned any details. Oedipus doesn't know that Laius was on his way to the oracle, or even that Laius was murdered, or that the Thebans never really investigated. Is there any wonder that he jumps to the conclusion that there was a conspiracy in Thebes to kill Laius (124–25)? And what about his precipitous marriage to the woman who proves to be his mother? Jocasta learns of Laius's death "just before" Oedipus arrives in Thebes – perhaps a day or so (736). So Oedipus comes to Thebes – looking remarkably like Laius, we are told (742–43) and with swollen feet; he solves the riddle of the sphinx then and marries Jocasta with no mention whatsoever of a mourning period? Oedipus knows that Laius is dead, but not dead *yesterday*. This version is a little tight on time, but at least the sequence seems right. However, considering the following, another version is possible:

Oedipus: Alas, these things are already apparent. Whoever was the one who spoke these words to you, wife?

Jocasta: A servant, who alone arrived having been saved.

Oedipus: Does he chance to be present now in the house?

Jocasta: No, when he came from that place, and saw your power, Laius having perished, taking hold of my hand, he entreated me to send him into the fields to take charge of pasturing the flocks so as to be especially out of sight of the town. And I did send him, for he is a worthy man, for a slave, deserving more thanks than this. (754–64)

This slave (the one who initially saved baby Oedipus) comes back from having seen Laius killed to find Oedipus and Jocasta *already* married. He sees a murderer of a certain age on the throne who looks remarkably like Laius, limps, and comes from Corinth. What does he do? He runs away, thus tacitly condoning bigamy (Jocasta learns of Laius's death only from him), regicide, parricide, and incest rather than admitting to a lie (the "many" robbers).

What are we to make of all of this? Did Oedipus kill Laius or not? Sophocles surely does not want you to say no; he rather wants you to realize that, although you do not really know, for the sake of making sense of the plot of the *Oedipus Tyrannus*, you feel compelled to assume Oedipus's "guilt." The *Oedipus Tyrannus* seems in general to allow for two sorts of interpretation. One turns on Oedipus's character, especially his anger; the plot is simply a useful vehicle to reveal this, and so we are inclined to glide over its various glitches. The other turns on the plot, and so these problems cannot be ignored. The question is how these two ways of reading the play are to be related. According to the first, Oedipus is a well-meaning man who, through no particular ambition of his own, has been named king of Thebes (he turns out to be quite a good one) and who is above all trying to avoid committing the most terrible of crimes. According to the second he is essentially defined as the doer of these crimes. This problem is revealed to us in a *double entendre* contained within the title of the play. In the fifth century B.C. when this play was first performed, *tyrannos* had come to mean "tyrant" – a man who seizes power illegitimately and governs without law. But in the mythic time at which the story of the play is supposed to be taking place, *tyrannos* would simply have meant "king." Playgoers would have been unable not to hear both meanings at once, and this in a way is the problem of the play. Oedipus the *tyrannos*, is a king whom we see immediately to be extraordinarily respected. He is a man who, because he performed a great public benefaction (solving the riddle and lifting the plague), was asked to rule. He proves to be a model of public spiritedness. He rather frequently reminds the Thebans of how much he feels their pain. On the other hand Oedipus the *tyrannos* is a tyrant who, in defiance of the most sacred prohibitions, kills his father, marries his mother, and brings a terrible plague on his city. How are we to think these two together? Why is Oedipus the good singled out to commit parricide and incest, especially since the chorus will identify him as a paradigm for the way in which mortals never have more than apparent happiness (ll. 89–92).

Now, to answer these questions fully would require an interpretation of the whole play. But the way to such an interpretation is already hinted at by the first words: *ô tekna* – "O offspring." Oedipus seems to begin by addressing his fellow Thebans as children. The next word – *kadmou* – alters this initial impression while still leaving it intact as a sort of aftershadow. He calls them not children (although he *will* do so some fifty lines later – 58), but children of Cadmus, the legendary founder of Thebes who, after slaying the local dragon, planted its teeth in the ground from which men grew. These plant-men fought each other until only seven remained – the aborigines of Thebes. So Oedipus begins by calling those who have come to ask his help (they include the old, the very young, and youths but no men in their prime) Thebans. He thus treats them as though he were their father; he places himself above them. This perhaps has something to do with why he was able to solve the riddle and so become their king. Oedipus, he of the swollen foot (*oidi pous*), comes to Thebes presumably relying on a staff for support. The man who figures out that the key to the riddle of the sphinx is the unfolding of human nature in time is at the same time the man who does not conform to his own description. As a man in his prime who uses a staff to support himself, he is an anomaly – an outsider who can see things more clearly because he is apart from what he is describing. Accordingly, the Thebans come to him for help almost as though he were a god. The priest who speaks at the beginning feels the need to tell Oedipus that they do not think him a god but only the "first of men," "most powerful to all," and certainly on very good terms with the gods (31–43). Even Oedipus sometimes seems to get his status a little confused. After making a proclamation concerning the still at large murderer of Laius, Oedipus stipulates what will happen if he is not obeyed.

> And to those not doing these things I pray the gods neither crop for them to come forth from the ground nor children from women . . . (269–71)

Of course this is simply a description of what is already the case in Thebes; it is the plague that the oracle of Apollo has indicated to be the punishment for not having brought Laius's murderer to justice. Oedipus thus confuses the consequences of the failure to heed the gods with the consequences of the failure to obey his decree.

Something of the character of this difficulty is revealed by the way Oedipus refers to the place on the road between Delphi and Thebes where the murder of Laius took place. Jocasta is the first to refer to it in the play. She calls it a place where three roads meet (714) and then a split road (733). She shows us that it is perfectly natural to refer to a fork in the road in either of these ways. But Oedipus always (four times, at 730, 800, 1398, 1399) refers to the site of the murder as a "triple way." It might be appropriate for Jocasta to refer to it as though she hovered above it; she knows this place only in thought and not by experience—for her it is a place on a map. But Oedipus clearly experienced it not as a triple way but as a fork in the road. When a road splits, one traveling down it is faced with *two* possibilities; retracing one's steps is ordinarily not an option. Oedipus tends to forget that he too is traveling down a road. He assumes for himself a perspectiveless knowledge.

Let us put the whole thing slightly differently. What the apparently quite simple, but actually quite dense, first sentence of the play indicates is that Oedipus is unaware that he too is a child of Cadmus. He is thus not only the father of the Thebans over whom he rules; he is also their brother. The very first three words of the *Oedipus Tyrannus* present us with an Oedipus who is guilty of incest. Now this is only a metaphor; a further interpretation would require that we think through what this guilt really means. Nevertheless, we have seen enough to know that Sophocles seems to mean for us to look for the "objective correlative" of Oedipus incest in his behavior as king. Without this we cannot understand the play, and yet it would never be apparent on a first reading; it becomes available only by chewing.

Good books provide countless examples of beginnings of comparable richness. Descartes begins the *Discourse on Method* – that clarion call to reason and founding document of the Enlightenment – with the following sentence:

> Good sense is of the things in the world the best apportioned; because everyone thinks himself to be so well provided with it that even those who are the most difficult to satisfy in every other thing are not at all accustomed to desire more of it than they have.

This is surely a joke. We are all equally rational because we are all equally vain? To spell out how this sentence is and is not a joke would be to provide an interpretation of the Discourse as a whole. Not until the end of Part 6 does Descartes provide you with enough information fully to understand his first sentence, in this way forcing any genuinely penetrating reading to be a rereading.

The first line of Plato's *Laches* is yet another case; it seems harmless enough. Lysimachus, a nobody who is the son of a famous statesman, has lured two well-respected contemporary generals, Laches and Nicias, to a display of a man fighting in armor. He means to use the occasion as a way to ask their advice first about whether this art is something his son should learn, and second how in general his son should be educated. At the end of the demonstration Lysimachus says, "You have seen the man fighting in armor." At first we accept this, but then we begin to wonder what on earth it means to see a man fighting all by himself. No doubt it was something like shadow-boxing, albeit in armor, but this has as much in common with dancing as it does with fighting, for the essential ingredient of fighting is missing – opposition. Later, after Socrates enters the dialogue, and begins manipulating everyone in sight, he will force the conversation from the general question of the education of the young to the specific question of what courage is. This is supposed to be an example of what one would have to know in order to know what virtue is, in order to know whom to choose as a teacher of one's sons. In fact, the choice of courage accomplishes two additional things: it guarantees that when the two famous generals reveal that they cannot even define the virtue that supposedly belongs to their concerns as generals they will be taken down a peg and exceedingly embarrassed, and it smuggles into the discussion the question of what it means to have the sort of inner strength that leads one to overcome the temptation to do what one thinks one should not do. This, of course, is the truth of the first sentence; we are to try to understand what it would mean to see *a* man fighting, which can only mean struggling with himself.

And then there are the first few sentences of Aristotle's *Nicomachean Ethics*:

> Every art and every inquiry, and similarly action (*praxis*) and intention, seem to aim at some good; hence the good has been beautifully called that at which all things aim. But a difference is apparent among ends; for some are activities (*energeiai*), while some are products (*erga*) apart from them. And of those in which the ends are something apart from the actions, in these the products (*erga*) are by nature better than the activities (*energeiai*).

Aristotle thus begins with an observation about particular kinds of human behavior – they each aim at what seems good. He then generalizes and draws the conclusion that *all things* aim at *the* good, and he calls the declaration of this generalization *kalon*, or beautiful – a conclusion (not expressed in Aristotle's own name) extravagant to the extent that to "*seem* to aim at *some* good" is not the same as to "*aim* at *the* good." The reason for the extravagance becomes clear in the sentences that follow. Aristotle first divides ends into two sorts: activities (*energeiai*) and products (*erga)* apart from the activities producing them; we dance and we make shoes. Then he seems simply to restate one side of the distinction as "those in which the ends are something apart from their actions (*praxeis*)." So actions (*praxeis*) divide into activities having their ends within them (here Aristotle is helped by the etymology of *en-ergeia*) and others with their *erga* apart from them. But he now adds "in these the *erga* are better than the *energeiai*." Now here *energeia* cannot have its etymological sense of having its product within itself; Aristotle can only be using it as a synonym for *praxis* – action. But this ambiguity not accidentally reflects the difficulty of the exaggerated conclusion of the first sentence.

We began with activities apparently perfectly complete in and of themselves; these are then quite literally transformed into activities understood as incomplete because having their products outside of themselves. Why the transformation? It occurs because we are in the midst of asking what these initially self-justifying activities are for. Or, it is the generalization about *the* good, which turns out to be happiness, that leads us to conclude that things originally seeming good to us cannot be simply good. We may make shoes in order to dance, but now we also dance in order to be happy. And we are moved to generalize in this way because we seek to *understand* what is good in the various goods of our experience. The underlying issue of the *Nicomachean Ethics* will be precisely the question of the effect on the good of attempting to understand the good, and accordingly what the good is of attempting to understand the good. This problem later shows itself in the tension between moral and intellectual virtue, within moral virtue as the tension between pride and justice, and still later as the tension between the account of friendship in Book 8 and that in Book 9. Yet it is already encoded in the first sentences of the *Nicomachean Ethics*. This is one of the many results of chewing that we do not and could not see on a first reading.

One final thing, surely, if any of what I have said about learning is true, it must have applications beyond texts narrowly understood. This is another way of asking why on earth someone like me has been asked to come to talk to you under the auspices of a department of anthropology. Let me end, therefore, not with an interpretation, but rather with a quotation that may perhaps make it a little clearer how this way of learning about learning might infect disciplines apart from philosophy and literature.

> An alien culture is inevitably a mystery and its comprehension can aptly be described as a piece of detective work. Baffling to

begin with, at times intriguing (though more often merely annoying), a culture reveals itself to even the most careful observer as a network of clues, usually misleading at first, and as gradual disclosures, at best only partly accurate.

These are the first two sentences of another book called *Sala'Ilua: A Samoan Mystery*, written some eighteen years ago by a then little-known anthropologist named Bradd Shore.[8]

8 Shore, Bradd, *Sala'Ilua: A Samoan Mystery* (New York: Columbia University Press, 1982), xiii-xiv.

Chapter 8

WHY I READ SUCH GOOD BOOKS: AESCHYLUS, SOPHOCLES, THE MORAL MAJORITY, AND SECULAR HUMANISM[1]

The inspiration for my title is the third section of Nietzsche's *Ecce Homo*; I'd like to work toward what it means in a very round about manner by way of Aeschylus's *Eumenides* and Sophocles' *Ajax*.

At the beginning of the *Ajax*, Achilles has just died. Since he was clearly superior to all the other Greek warriors, and since the goal of a warrior is "to be the best and preeminent among men," the question for the Greeks becomes, Who is now best? Despite the acknowledged superiority of Ajax as a fighter – he is *the* great defensive warrior among them and a man who accepts no help from the gods – they award Achilles' armor to the wily Odysseus – the man Athena is *always* helping. Faced with their decision, Ajax goes mad and sets out at night to slaughter the whole of the Greek army as it sleeps. Athena clouds his vision and makes him think that the herds the Greeks have captured and use for supplies are the army. Ajax slaughters them all and drags some animals back to his tent,

1 Originally presented in the fall of 1981 as part of the Fantasy Lecture Series organized by students at Sarah Lawrence College.

thinking that among them are Odysseus, Agamemnon, and Menelaus. After torturing them, he awakens from his delusion to discover what he has done. Ajax then commits suicide. The question of the play now becomes whether the Greeks will allow Ajax's corpse to be buried. Menelaus and Agamemnon are about to refuse him burial when Odysseus intervenes on Ajax's behalf, and they relent.

The immediate problem for any audience of the *Ajax* is to understand this madness. Its meaning first began to become clearer to me when I asked myself why Ajax had to kill himself; that is, why couldn't he simply go back and do it right this time? That he does not make a second attempt means that he must consider the failure of his first attempt in some way final and without remedy. But why should this be?

Let's step back a bit to remind ourselves of what we know about Ajax. He is the hero who scorns the help of the gods on the grounds that virtue is not virtue if it requires divine assistance. This clearly also means that virtue is not virtue if it depends on chance. Accordingly, when Ajax loses the contest for Achilles' armor to Odysseus and when he fails to kill the army in revenge, he cannot attribute his failure to bad luck or misunderstanding. This is why those who awarded the armor to Odysseus, the Greek army, necessarily become his enemies. When his situation is understood in this way, Ajax's only possible course of action is to attempt to punish them. Failing in that attempt, he has proved himself not to be best, and so kills himself.

Now, Ajax is saved from an act of extraordinary brutality only because Athena causes him to see the Greek herds as the Greeks. In so doing she has made visible to us his characteristic defect: Ajax cannot tell the difference between men and beasts. Or more exactly, since he kills not only the herds but the human herdsmen attending them, where others would see a distinction between beast and man, Ajax sees only the human. But what does this mean? The human, as opposed to the subhuman, is the purposive – the intentional; our world is a world in which things are done for reasons. Accordingly, the human response to an event is to ask, Why? If this question were always to receive an answer, this would amount to the elimination of chance. And in a world in which there is no chance, the appropriate response to opposition is anger. The *Ajax* is, therefore, a play about the absolute character of enmity in a world that is entirely purposive.

What seems at first strange is that it is only in this entirely "human" or secular world that enmity can be so brutal, for if there is only chance, then all harm is unintentional and so undeserving of anger. Of course, in such a world it would make no sense to long to be "best and preeminent." A world in which everything is intentional, in which everything is governed by purposes, is a world of extreme brutality. A world in which chance governs altogether is meaningless. The solution to this dilemma? The gods. The gods provide an order in which purposes govern, but because this order is not fully known, the experience of it is not so very different from the experience of chance. Their presence thus prevents us from taking our own purposes, our human purposes, as absolute.

The beginning of the *Ajax* thus sketches for us the following problem. We need the gods but for reasons other than we are first inclined to think – not because they are necessary to keep us moral but rather because without them we are *too* moral, too righteous. And the result of this righteousness is the most extreme brutishness. Ajax's complete devotion to the human is only a hair's breadth from an attempt to annihilate the human altogether.

Let's leave Sophocles for a moment and turn to Aeschylus. The *Eumenides* is the last play of the *Oresteia*, a trilogy that begins with the *Agamemnon* and the *Libation Bearers*. Agamemnon leads an army to Troy (the same army as in the *Ajax*) to avenge the theft of Helen, the wife of his brother, Menelaus. The Greek fleet assembles at Aulis, but unfavorable winds prevent it from sailing. Agamemnon is told by a priest that he will not be able to sail until he sacrifices his daughter, Iphigeneia, to Artemis. He does so, the Greeks sail against Troy, and after a war of ten years they are victorious. When Agamemnon returns, he is murdered by his wife, Clytemestra, and her lover, Aegisthus. The immediate events leading up to this murder are the story of the Agamemnon. In the next play, the *Libation Bearers*, Orestes, the son of Agamemnon and Clytemestra, avenges his father and kills his mother and Aegisthus. This takes us to the final play, the *Eumenides*, in which Orestes is pursued by avenging deities – the Furies. These goddesses were mentioned in Greek literature prior to Aeschylus, but he seems to have given them the characteristics attributed to them in all subsequent stories – both their physical characteristics and their job as avengers of blood crimes – crimes against the family. The Furies follow Orestes to Delphi, where he is purified by Apollo, whose oracle had at least strongly suggested that he kill his mother. Apollo then sends Orestes to Athens, where Athena uses his case to establish the first jury trial in Athens. The Furies prosecute, Apollo is the defense attorney, Orestes the defendant, Athena the judge, and a group of Athenian citizens comprises the jury. The verdict is to acquit, with Athena voting to force the jury into a tie. Orestes is declared innocent and goes home to Argos. Athena compensates the Furies by giving them a home in Athens and a new job description; they will be now in charge of childbirth and the weather.

The play is strange and full of puzzles. If we identify the founding of Athenian democracy with the founding of the court of the Areopagus, why should Aeschylus connect this founding to a trial outside the jurisdiction of Athens (Orestes is far from his native Argos) in which the jury never hears the relevant evidence (for example, they know nothing of Iphigeneia), and in which both prosecution and defense attempt to bribe and threaten them? And what is the connection between establishing a jury system and providing a new home and job for the Furies?

Now, it would take a long story to address these issues adequately, but a few things can be said.[2] Aeschylus sees that a jury system in which you feel guilt when you make a mistake is impossible – fear of error would lead you to find everyone innocent. He therefore gives as the first example of a jury trial nothing noble but rather a farce in which there is no question of having genuinely considered the issue. That the jury is almost evenly split means that, no matter

---

2 It is a story well told by Seth Benardete, from whom a good deal of this analysis is borrowed. See his "The *Furies* of Aeschylus," in *The Argument of the Action*.

what the correct judgment ought to have been, in this trial half of the jurors will have been wrong. This is somehow the paradigmatic trial, for human justice is fallible justice. True in court, this is also true within political life generally. Political life requires that you take your positions seriously; you must think that you are right. If you vote for Orestes, you are siding with Apollo, and if you vote against him you are siding with the Furies. In either case, you are voting for a god, and having made such a serious commitment, you are not likely to sit idly by and watch the opposition win regardless of the final vote.

This problem is the fundamental problem of democracy. All votes are equal; you are meant to vote according to your conscience. Yet if all votes are equal, why do 51% of the voters override 49%? So all votes, or positions, are not equal. Democracy is only possible because of a prior unanimous agreement to obey the rule of the majority, and this means that you are not to take your principles – your god – too seriously. You must separate the holy from the just, for if you do not, the resulting unbending adherence to the holy will ultimately lead to civil war. Aeschylus's view, then, would seem to be that it is necessary to remove the gods from political life for the sake of avoiding the most extreme brutality. This is the significance of placing matters in the hands of human jurors.

Where does all of this leave us? Aeschylus's view is that the presence of the gods within political life leads to brutality. Sophocles' view is that removing the gods from political life leads to brutality. Tragedy is in a way built on this problem. Political and moral life both needs and cannot have the gods within it. There is a secular version of this problem. To make a law, any law, one must weigh its potential goodness and badness. The measure of the goodness of a law cannot itself be legal; it must be translegal in some sense. One must go beyond the law in order to make the law, yet as soon as the law is made it must stand as the measure of what is to be done. The law must be and cannot be the highest authority.

Neither Aeschylus nor Sophocles is unaware of this paradox; indeed, both sides of the issue are present in both plays. But I want to return to matters of more immediate concern to us. It should by now be clear that the terms of the arguments in these two plays are not so very different from the terms of the contemporary debate between secular humanism and the moral majority. But Aeschylus and Sophocles reveal a depth to the problem that would never have emerged from a reflection on the contemporary debate. The theological-political problem is that healthy politics needs and cannot have the gods. Without them we have no common standards and cannot live together; with them our standards are so uncompromising as to make it impossible to live together.

Now, why did I bring all of this up – i.e., why do I read such good books? Liberal education is supposed to be liberating. It is supposed to free us from prejudices by forcing us to question the things we take most for granted. To seek for its immediate and obvious relevance is simply to give in to our deepest and most hidden prejudices. "Learning by doing" means simply to forget to ask what you are doing. The much maligned ivory tower has a great deal to be said for it, for if you really want to understand the battle between the secular humanists and the moral majoritarians, you might begin by reading Aeschylus and Sophocles.

Chapter 9

PLATO AND NIETZSCHE ON DEATH: AN INTRODUCTION TO THE *PHAEDO*[1]

The title of this paper is something of a lie – a noble lie, but still a lie[2] – for I will not treat Plato and Nietzsche equally in what follows. Still, the title reflects one of the crucial problems of contemporary philosophy and of contemporary life. For those who would like to be Platonists Nietzsche represents the most difficult obstacle. His critique of Platonism, a critique which runs from his earliest to his latest works, is powerful. For modern man, to come to terms with Platonism means to come to terms with Nietzsche. In this sense Nietzsche is present throughout what follows.

I

The contest between Plato and Nietzsche is more than academic. If Socrates was for Nietzsche the "one vortex and turning point of so-called world history,"[3] Plato was surely the Napoleon of this

---

1 With a few small variations this lecture was originally presented at Wesleyan University in the spring of 1978 and later published in *Ancient Philosophy* (Vol. 1, No. 1, Fall 1980, 69–80). All translations from the *Phaedo* are my own and are based on Burnet's edition (Oxford: 1989). References to Nietzsche are to Karl Schlechta's edition, *Friedrich Nietzsche: Werke in Drei Bänden* (Munich: Carl Hanser Verlag, 1966), hereafter cited as *Nietzsche*. I have followed Walter Kaufmann's translations from the German with occasional corrections of my own.

2 See *Nietzsche* II, 982.

Socratic revolution. It may be that with Socrates "Greek taste changes in favor of dialectics,"[4] but it is Plato who imposes Greek taste on the West. For Nietzsche the West is in some sense the Christian West, and "Christianity is Platonism for the people."[5] It is Plato who is responsible for the transformation of the "true world" into a fable, although in him, Nietzsche admits, the fable is still "relatively sensible, simple and persuasive."[6] Nietzsche characterizes Platonism as the self-glorification of the sage.[7] About the sage Nietzsche's Zarathustra has this to say:

> His wisdom is: to wake in order to sleep well. And verily if life had no sense, and I had to choose nonsense, then I too would choose this the most sensible form of nonsense.[8]

The contest between Plato and Nietzsche is, according to Nietzsche, a contest between the view that really makes sense of life and "the most sensible form of nonsense," that is, between truth and the most seductive form of error. To understand Nietzsche's attack on Plato in even the most provisional way means to understand this Platonic seductiveness.

At first glance this seems rather difficult. However, we must remember that the same Nietzsche who says "Plato is boring"[9] also says that Plato "becomes a caricature in my hands."[10] This caricature is fairly clear. Plato is the chief among those otherworldly ones. He seeks to interpret this world in terms of another world; in his hands the real things of this world become mere copies of things in the other world, and this life becomes a preparation for another. This life and this world cannot help but suffer in comparison to a higher world and higher life. The suffering is two-fold; the world becomes both bad and unintelligible. Plato seems to say that it is bad because it is unintelligible; Nietzsche seems to say that this identification of the good with the intelligible is an example of Platonic cowardice.

3 *Nietzsche* I, 85.
4 *Nietzsche* II, 953.
5 *Nietzsche* II, 566.
6 *Nietzsche* II, 963.
7 *Nietzsche* II, 963.
8 *Nietzsche* II, 296–97.
9 *Nietzsche* II, 1028.
10 *Nietzsche* III, 596.

> Plato is a coward before reality, consequently he flees into the ideal; "Thucydides has control of *himself*, consequently he has control of things.[11]

Thus Nietzsche claims that

> About life, the wisest of all ages have judged the same: it is worthless.[12]

The wise slander life in the name of some higher standard. This "faithlessness to the earth" is the basis of all "improvement moralities" and is behind what Nietzsche describes in the title of the third section of his *Twilight of the Idols* – "HOW THE 'TRUE' WORLD FINALLY BECAME A FABLE: The History of an Error." That Nietzsche thinks it an error that the world should become a fable is clear, but thus far it is by no means clear what tempts men to forsake this life on the hope of another. Just what is it that is so seductive about Plato's error? To find out we must penetrate Nietzsche's caricature.

The most obvious answer is that hope of another life allows us to overcome our greatest fear. The hope of immortality calms our fear of death. Platonism is non-popular Christianity in that it provides the metaphysical foundations for the hope of a life to come. *The* source for this view of Plato is the *Phaedo*, the dialogue that gives us an account of the dying Socrates, an account of how Socrates faces, and apparently overcomes, his fear of death. The simplest explanation for Socrates' ability to overcome his fear of death is that he too believes in the immortality of the soul. Because he believes in a life after death, he does not fear death. Nietzsche, himself, saw that this is not really the way of the *Phaedo*. It is a sort of fable.

> Is Plato's integrity beyond question? – But we know at least that he wanted to have taught as absolute truth what he himself did not even regard as conditionally true: namely the separate existence and particular immortality of "souls."[13]

11 *Nietzsche* II, 1029.
12 *Nietzsche* II, 951.
13 *Nietzsche* III, 757–58.

Nietzsche apparently does not consider Plato "relatively sensible, simple and persuasive" for his teaching regarding the immortality of souls. If we wish to understand the nature of Plato's most sensible form of nonsense, we will have to get beyond the most obvious level of the *Phaedo*. This will require an explanation for the dialogue's apparent concern for the immortality of the soul. We will then have to look in some non-obvious places for the dialogue's true concern.

II

Let us suppose that Nietzsche is right, that Plato does not regard the separate existence and particular immortality of souls even as conditionally true.[14] Then why does he teach it as "absolute truth?" To begin to answer this question means to reflect on the nature of a Platonic *dialogue* as a dramatic presentation of philosophical argumentation. That is, something usually understood as neither having nor needing a context is intentionally embedded within a context. The context of the *Phaedo* cries out for attention. Socrates is in prison awaiting his death. The *Phaedo* is his discussion of immortality in his last meeting with his friends before his own death. But perhaps "friends" is too strong a word. With the exception of Crito (and there are indications that what Socrates says has very little effect on Crito), those present are admirers of Socrates and of philosophy – they do not always distinguish very clearly between the two. The best of Socrates' followers, if we may judge Plato to be the best, is not present. Plato is sick.[15] It is clear from the narrative

14 That this supposition is correct would require a separate analysis of each of the arguments of the *Phaedo* in their contexts, a task beyond the scope of this essay. I have attempted part of such an analysis in my "Socrates' Pre-Socratism: Some Remarks on the Structure of Plato's *Phaedo*," *Review of Metaphysics*, vol. 33, no. 131, March 1980, 559–77. One gets a hint of Plato's real view by putting together the only definition of death ever offered in the *Phaedo* – the separation of soul from body (64c) – with the claim at 105e that the soul does not admit death. The result seems to be that the soul does not admit the separation of soul from body. I am grateful to Seth Benardete for this observation.

15 Plato's absence is important for at least two reasons. First, it pretty much silences those who take Platonic dialogues to be essentially recordings of actual conversations. Plato can hardly have recorded a conversation that he makes a point of telling us he never heard (it is interesting that while the structure of the *Phaedo* suggests that part of the intent in celebrating the death of Socrates is to

structure of the *Phaedo* that what Socrates says on this last day of his life will have a lasting effect on those present and on others who are not present. Like the *Symposium*, which is also narrated by one of those present at the death of Socrates, the *Phaedo* is eagerly told and eagerly listened to. Also like the *Symposium*, it is a dialogue that recounts Socrates' almost superhuman powers. Socrates' calm in the face of the greatest of human fears is an example to those young men who follow him more powerful than any of the proofs he presents for the immortality of the soul. Those present may or may not be convinced by these proofs, but they cannot fail to be impressed by Socrates' fearlessness.

The *Phaedo* moves on several levels. On the level of argumentation it provides a series of proofs for the immortality of the soul. None of these proofs bear up under close examination, although the reasons why they fail are themselves instructive. On the dramatic level, that Socrates offers proofs for the immortality of the soul means that he thinks those present need them, that they are still not rid of the "little child in them." On this dramatic level Plato indicates a parallel between Socrates and Theseus, who, we are told, saved fourteen Athenian youths and maidens from the dreaded Minotaur (58a–b). Shortly thereafter Phaedo gives an enumeration of those present at Socrates' death, and we discover that fourteen youths are present. Like Theseus, Socrates will save these youths from a dreaded monster. While it is not in his power to save them from death, he can save them from the fear of death. The most obvious way to do so is to convince them that they will not die, and this is the most obvious intent of the *Phaedo*.[16] Human beings live better lives when they are not continually haunted by the knowledge of the necessity of their own deaths. On this level the *Phaedo* as a whole performs the function normally attributed to myth. Indeed, throughout the

confer a kind of immortality on him, Plato's self-announced absence makes us wonder whether it is the real Socrates who is being immortalized). Secondly, that Plato's reason for absenting himself is sickness has a special irony. To stay home because you are sick suggests that ultimately some value is being placed on staying alive. This is of course contrary to what Socrates explicitly seems to claim in the *Phaedo*. Here again I am indebted to Seth Benardete.

16 Compare *Republic* 386a–88e.

Phaedo Socrates consistently refers to their conversation in words that liken it to myth.[17]

But this cannot be the only level of the *Phaedo*. It is not simply a noble lie. Just as in the *Symposium* there is a link between the lowest manifestation of *eros* and its highest manifestation, so that the high is prefigured in the low, so also the fear of death that finds some comfort in the hope of not dying is a prefiguring of something higher. One may state the problem this way. Socrates' proofs for the immortality of the soul may not be adequate or even seriously offered, but his calm in the face of death remains a fact. If the teaching of the *Phaedo* is not the immortality of the soul, it still remains for us to ask after the source of the power of this Socratic calm and to ask as well how it is connected to the common view of immortality. With that we must turn to what I take to be the real issue of Plato's *Phaedo*.

III

The first word of the *Phaedo* is *autos* – self; the problem of the dialogue is the problem of the self. One might say this is equally true of the *Philebus*, *Symposium*, or *Phaedrus*, to mention only a few dialogues. The *Phaedo* differs from these dialogues in that it deals with the problem of the self from the perspective of that problem most difficult *for* the self – the problem of death. One cannot discuss death apart from a discussion of life. For Plato this means a discussion of soul, or *psuchê*. It is therefore no surprise that the *Phaedo* should bear the alternative title *Peri Psuchês* – *Concerning Soul*. Still, the *Phaedo* will be concerned with a particular kind of soul – one that not only dies but has knowledge of the inevitability of its own eventual death. This kind of soul, unlike the soul of a tree or the soul of a dog, knows that it is a soul. It is appropriate that the *Phaedo* should begin with the intensive pronoun *autos*. The beginning immediately alerts us to the hardest problem of the dialogue – the nature of the soul that knows *itself* to be a soul, or the nature of life that knows itself to be alive. Such a soul necessarily purchases self-knowledge at the price of knowledge of its own mortality. It

17 See, for example, 61b–c, 61e, 70b, and 110a–b.

must therefore be considered from two perspectives – as something that lives and dies and as something that knows. The *Phaedo* uses the occasion of the death of Socrates to consider the human soul from both perspectives and to reveal a tension between the two.

The *Phaedo* is narrated by Phaedo to a man named Echecrates. Both are interested in hearing or rehearing the story of the death of Socrates. Nevertheless there is an interesting discrepancy in their motives. Echecrates wants to know what Socrates said on his last day and how he died (57a). He later repeats his wish to hear what was *said* and *done* (58c). Phaedo, who claims that his greatest pleasure comes from remembering Socrates, replies by saying first what was done; only after he is asked again to repeat the speeches that were made does he begin what makes up the bulk of the dialogue. The difference in the concerns of the two men is understated, but it is present. A similar difference in emphasis recurs within the narrative itself. Of Socrates' two principle interlocutors, one, Cebes, is characterized as someone who is always on the track of *logoi* – speeches (63a), while the other, Simmias, repeatedly shows himself to be more concerned with the fate of Socrates than with the fate of the *logos* (63a, 76b–c, etc.). Plato seems intent on showing that there are two ways of approaching the death of Socrates. One is concerned more with the peculiarities of a particular man, with the personality, the self, Socrates. The other is concerned with what is ostensibly not peculiar to Socrates at all, at least not in principle – i.e., what he says. We are of course familiar with these two concerns. They are what make it possible to like people without admiring them and admire them without liking them. They are what make us interested not only in the argument of the *Critique of Pure Reason* or *Philosophical Investigations* but also in anecdotes about how the housewives of Königsberg were wont to set their clocks by Kant's morning walk and about how Wittgenstein once washed the dinner dishes in Norman Malcolm's bathtub. We may characterize the one as philosophy and the other as gossip, but this does not alter the fact that we are frequently as interested in the gossip as in the philosophy. Plato is at great pains to show us that the two are essentially connected in the human soul. Their connection is what makes it possible to talk about a self at all. We cannot of course ignore the fact that the idiosyncrasies of Wittgenstein's habits of cleaning up after dinner are not on a par with the idiosyncratic aspects of Socrates' death. One supposes there is something especially revealing about the way a man dies. In sum, Plato goes out of his way to show us two approaches to Socrates, and so to the death of Socrates, and so to death simply. A Platonic dialogue is particularly well suited to show this duality since in it arguments are attached to people and not disembodied as they seem to be in a treatise.

More precisely, how does the problem of death serve to reveal this essential duality of the human soul? How does the knowledge of the necessity of our own deaths reveal our natures? The result of that knowledge is generally fear, not the fear we feel when faced with an immediate and obvious danger. This sort of fear is predictable and so to speak one-dimensional. The *Phaedo* is concerned with a different fear of death, what Cebes calls "the child in us who has such fears" (77e). Whatever is in us mortals that allows us to anticipate our own deaths, an event that we do not in any ordinary way experience, also allows us to imagine ourselves as in some way continuing after death. The mortal fear of death naturally gives rise to a longing for immortality as its cure. This longing is not a desire to be different from what we are; it is rather a desire to remain eternally what we already are. It is an attachment to *ourselves*. It is also a desire to *know* that we will remain eternally as we are. Only knowledge of our own immortality can destroy the fears of that child in us and, in a rather radical way, force it to grow up. But what accompanies this sudden maturity? Would it not substantially change us, not simply in superficial ways but in important ways? Wouldn't particular desires and pleasures cease to have the urgency they have for a mortal being if we were to become immortal and thus possess the potentiality for experiencing the same desires and pleasures an infinite number of times? Wouldn't this change the character of the desire radically or perhaps even annihilate it altogether? If so, in what sense can our original longing for immortality be said to have been fulfilled? In what sense have we remained eternally as we are? In what sense can we even recognize ourselves as the same? Or, in what sense is the original self retained in this new immortal self? The desire of the self for its own immortality seems to be a concealed death wish (there are, of course, others who have made this connection between *eros* and *thanatos*).

That Plato is aware of this difficulty for the ordinary view of immortality is clear from his treatment of pleasure and pain in the *Phaedo*. Phaedo is the first to mention pleasure (58e). He says that it is his greatest pleasure to be reminded of Socrates. He then describes his feelings on the day of Socrates' death as a strange mixture of pleasure, because they were occupied with philosophy, and pain, because Socrates was about to die (59a). Socrates himself turns to this problematic togetherness of pleasure and pain close to the beginning of the narration.

> "How odd," he said, "men, a thing this seems to be which human beings call pleasant. How wondrously it is by nature related to its seeming opposite, the painful, so that on the one hand they will not both come to be present together in one human being, but on the other hand, if someone pursues the one and take it, he would almost be compelled also to take the other, as though the two were held together from one head. And it seems to me," he said, "if Aesop had considered them, he would have composed a myth – how, wanting to reconcile them when they were at war, when he was unable, the god joined their heads together into the same head, and for these reasons, when one comes to be present to someone, the other also follows along after. So too then for me myself it seems to be, when the painful was in my leg owing to the fetter, the pleasant appears to have come following along after." (60b–c)

Let us see if we can make out the connection between the question of pleasure and pain and the question of death. Pleasure is better than pain. All things considered, it would be better to have all pleasure and no pain. This attempt to maximize pleasure is the structure of human action. It is not hedonism in any pejorative sense but merely the common-sensical view that what we all desire is happiness. Pain makes us unhappy, and so when we try to imagine perfect happiness, there is no room for pain in it. But if pleasure and pain are really coupled together as this Socratic fable suggests, the complete absence of pain would be possible only given the complete absence of pleasure. The natural desire to maximize pleasure, if pushed to its extreme, is a sort of death wish. Socrates' pleasure was a result of being released from his fetters; it depended on his having been bound. It is therefore doubtful whether it makes sense for human beings to talk about a perfect pleasure, i.e., a complete release from fetters. If we make the connection indicated at 67b–c between being freed from our bodies, we – i.e., our *selves* – can never really be freed from our bodies. It appears that Nietzsche was correct. Plato does not really regard as true either the separate existence or the immortality of the soul.

The perspective of common sense, for which the fear of death is the greatest pain and complete satisfaction with no admixture of pain is the greatest pleasure, requires the separate existence and immortality of a certain kind of soul – one for which it still makes sense to provide a name. Common sense takes as its standard the soul, or life, as it is, and then attempts to imagine what would be the most satisfactory form of such a life. The result is an ideal life, which because it takes its bearings by the extreme – i.e., it *is* ideal – cannot be lived. The ideal version of life is incompatible with life; it turns out to be a kind of death. This is the tragedy of common sense. My attachment to my life simply because it is mine (this is the analogue to Simmias's attachment to Socrates as Socrates) is in principle tragic. The tragedy cannot be avoided by simply ignoring the extreme view. While it is the case that the tragedy does not exist for a mollusk, it is also the case that a mollusk does not know that it is a mollusk. The human self seems to be constituted by the conflict between its desire to be what it is and its desire to be other than what it is. The tragedy is that both desires seem to spring from the very same source.

Of the two aspects of the human soul that account for the duality of approach to the death of Socrates in the *Phaedo*, the second is introduced as an inversion of the view of common sense. Cebes is its representative. He forgets him*self* in the argument, or at least attempts to minimize the effect that self will have on the argument. (Notice, however, that he engages in the argument for himself, for his own satisfaction. The particular self, even when its activity is understood as thinking, as *noêsis*, seems necessarily concerned with its own *noêsis*.) It is this sort of behavior Socrates has in mind when he characterizes philosophy as nothing but the practice of dying and being dead. This description of philosophy causes the practical Simmias to laugh because it is precisely what the common view is of philosophy – that not only do philosophers desire death but that they deserve it as well. Socrates' response is that the common view is correct; it simply doesn't go far enough. It does not understand in what way philosophers desire or deserve death or what sort of death it is that they desire and deserve. Philosophy begins from an awareness of the tragedy of common sense. The view of common sense that desires the preservation of the self at any cost destroys itself. The only suitable cost for immortality turns out to be the very self that was to have been preserved. This uncommon view, on the other hand, begins with the bold assertion that we ought to pursue death. We must of course ask why.

Socrates' first set of answers to this question (64c–65a) consists of a series of disparaging remarks about the pleasures and needs of the body. While this may seem typically Socratic, it is not justified here unless one takes into consideration the fact that we have already seen the self-destructive character of the ordinary desires of ordinary human beings. Perhaps the deepest of these desires, the desire for immortal life, if fulfilled would lead to a condition incompatible with life. The unimpeded pursuit of life represents a misunderstanding of life; perhaps the pursuit of death is the necessary antidote. Since we are in the midst of paradoxes of almost Nietzschean proportions, perhaps the pursuit of death in some as yet undefined manner is *the* condition for living well.

This would certainly be in keeping with Socrates' quick analysis of the virtues at 67d–69e. The gist of this analysis is that ordinary courage is not really courage. Courage is overcoming one's fear, but when we overcome our fear out of a still greater fear, whether of dishonor or of punishment, this can hardly be called courage. It is really a convoluted form of cowardice. And if we are moderate out of a desire for still greater pleasures we can hardly be said to be moderate (this argument is reminiscent of Zarathustra's view of chastity – that it may be a virtue in some but is almost a vice in many since those who pride themselves on it too highly are really lecherous in placing such emphasis on sexuality[18]). This argument

18 *Nietzsche* II, 318–19.

about the virtues can be extended to Socrates' own description of philosophy as the practice of death. If it is practiced as an escape from life, philosophy would be like the vulgar form of courage; the escape from life would be in the service of another life. In that case, Simmias and Cebes would be right in accusing Socrates of forsaking his masters here for others in some other life who are no better (62d–e). To face death means to face it as something different from another event in a life that does not really end after we are dead. If vulgar courage is just another form of fear, then turning death into another form of life is just a vulgar form of facing death.

For this reason it is of some importance that the whole question of immortality does not enter Socrates' argument as a means to overcome death. It enters as a means to overcome ignorance. It is because the body is a hindrance to *philo-sophia* – to love of wisdom – that Socrates is moved to speak of the desirability of the separation of body and soul at death. To the extent that bodily faculties are involved in a kind of knowing, this knowing is necessarily impure and so does not satisfy our love of wisdom. But why is it impure? The contamination of the body has to do with the fact that the body needs nourishment, that it must look to its own needs. It is subject to disease and, we might add, to the limit case of disease, death. Again, it must look to its own good. The body "fills us with loves, desires, and fears" that make it all but impossible to think. Finally, the body and its desires are the producers of war, factions and battles (66b–c). There is war only where there are conflicting interests. The body is the indication and the location of our own interests, of whatever it is that causes us to be concerned with *ourselves*. It is this self-concern that gets in the way of our pursuit of wisdom. Our desires and needs as particular selves color the way in which we look at the world. To see the world as it is and not through the lens of our *self*-interest requires neutralizing self-interest. It is not a careless use of the language when Nietzsche calls a similar attack on the passions by Christianity "castratism." It is "an attack on the roots of passion" which "means an attack on the roots of life."[19] The body is the home of self-interest in that its needs are most obviously its own. My hunger sets me at odds with you. My

19 *Nietzsche* II, 965.

pleasure satisfies me and not you. That we have bodies is the sign that our interests are not identical. That our interests are not identical is another way of saying that we are discernibly different selves. Were our interests to coincide completely, it is difficult to see what would distinguish us from each other.

This self-interestedness, of which the body is the most obvious sign, accounts for my *love* of wisdom (a selfish desire) but closes off the possibility of wisdom. For this reason, if death is the separation of the body from the soul, it is something to be desired. To be sure that its knowledge was not tainted the soul would have to exist itself by itself (*autê kath'autên*). Knowing would thus seem to be impossible while we are alive and only conceivable after we are dead. Wisdom is incompatible with life. The love of wisdom, or philosophy, thus consists in pursuing the opposite of life – death.

That is where this inversion of common sense seems to take us. There is, of course, an obvious objection. That life is incompatible with wisdom does not mean that death is compatible with wisdom. Perhaps wisdom is simply impossible. Socrates not only anticipates this objection, he invites it. He restates the conclusion several times (66e, 67e, etc.), and each time he is careful not to say that wisdom can be had but only that if it can be had, it can be had only after we die. So he intentionally provokes his interlocutors – Simmias on behalf of life and Cebes on behalf of wisdom – and his future listeners – Phaedo, Echecrates, and us. He does so to pose the problem of the human soul divided against itself in its desire to know and its desire to live. It is quite literally a life or death issue.

This is the deeper issue of the *Phaedo*. The problem cannot be resolved by separating off the soul from the body because it is not at all clear that there is a self left after that separation. Whatever soul might be understood to remain is not such as to have desires and interests that are peculiarly its own. Nor is the soul that is left after the separation the same as the soul that philosophizes. We who desire wisdom cannot be satisfied by wisdom because the conditions that are necessary for wisdom are incompatible with the existence of the self. Thus to say that philosophy consists in the practice of dying and being dead is really only to say that philosophy radicalizes the question of human life to such a point that it can ask not just which life is best but whether life as such can be good. On the apparent level of the *Phaedo*, where the issue remains immortality, the notion of a life after death performs the following function. By asserting the existence of a better life after death, this life is made better. That is, by providing a vantage point from which to judge the goodness of life, the character of this life can be known more fully. Still, if this vantage point is an illusion, what has been accomplished? The value of this life has been sacrificed out of a futile longing for wisdom.

To return to the question with which we began, Nietzsche finds Plato seductive because he shares with him this understanding of the fundamental duality of the human soul. That there is a tension between life and wisdom is acknowledged in the earliest of Nietzsche's works.

> Therefore Lessing, the most honest theoretical man, dared declare that he cared more for the search for truth than for the truth itself – and thus uncovered the fundamental secret of science, to the astonishment, even anger, of the scientific.[20]

But Nietzsche's Zarathustra is perhaps most eloquent on the point when he addresses his "wild wisdom."

> From the ground up I love only life – and truly then, most when I hate it! But that I am well disposed toward wisdom and often too well, that happens because she reminds me so much of life.[21]

Nietzsche finds Plato seductive because the two agree that the tension between life and wisdom is at once the most difficult and the most dangerous problem for men. Plato at least sees the problem even if, for Nietzsche, his way of solving it is the beginning of the characteristic error of the West.

Plato's error is that he chooses to judge life at all. Faced with the tension between life and wisdom, wisdom must yield. Again Nietzsche:

20 *Nietzsche* I, 84.
21 *Nietzsche* II, 365.

> One must by all means stretch out one's fingers and make the attempt to grasp this amazing finesse, *that the value of life cannot be estimated.* Not by the living, for they are an interested party, even a bone of contention and not judges; not by the dead on other grounds.[22]

To judge life presumes the very kind of detachment from life the lack of which caused us to judge life to be so bad. But we love life deeply most of all when we hate life. The living cannot help affirming life, and so

> From the vantage of a philosopher to see a problem in the *value* of life remains to this extent even an objection against him, a question mark concerning his wisdom, an unwisdom.[23]

If we take this to be the deepest level of Nietzsche's objection to Plato – and in a contest of this sort one must always be wary of speaking about the "deepest level" – there is still something to be said on Plato's behalf. Doesn't Nietzsche's judgment of those who judge life itself constitute a judgment of life? Put differently, if it is true that Nietzsche agrees that the human soul is essentially dual, and that its duality is constituted by its character as living and as knowing, then how is our humanity preserved in the denial of one half of the duality? Isn't Nietzsche as guilty of destroying the self in the name of some improvement morality as Plato is? If the history of the West is the story of how the true world became a fable, Nietzsche appears to turn the "true world" into a fable of a fable. In his affirmation of life he undermines the tension that supports life. He is a preacher of death. For reasons like these Heidegger has called the anti-metaphysical Nietzsche "the last metaphysician of the west."[24]

IV

Nietzsche's critique of Plato is that at the deepest level Plato is a nihilist. In the context of the *Phaedo*, this means that Plato finally cannot say what the source is of Socrates' power to face death.

---

22 *Nietzsche* II, 951–52.
23 *Nietzsche* II, 952.
24 Martin Heidegger, *Nietzsche I*, (Pfullingen: Verlag Guenther Neske, 1961), 480.

This is, of course, Nietzsche's view. I would like to sketch out what seem to me to be the general directions of Plato's view. The problem to be solved is this. To be good, human life requires philosophy – the love and pursuit of wisdom. But the conditions for wisdom are identical with the conditions for death. Philosophy is thus the pursuit of death; it is quite literally self-destructive. For Plato, the solution is a sort of compromise. We get a hint of it early in the dialogue. Socrates interrupts the conversation to see what his old friend Crito has been trying to tell him.

> "What else," said Crito, "than that for a long time the man who is to give you the poison has been saying to me that I ought to tell you to converse [*dialegesthai*] as little as possible. For he says those who converse grow more hot, and nothing of that sort must be brought to bear on the poison, lest those doing something of the sort be compelled to drink it twice or even thrice. (63d–e)

Socrates is predictably unconcerned and goes on talking. Several things are notable about this exchange. The verb used for "to converse" – *dialegesthai* – is frequently used by Plato in a more technical sense to mean dialectic – that same dialectic that Nietzsche says "one chooses only when one has no other means."[25] The reference in the passage to heat is interesting because later in the dialogue a connection will be made between heat and life (100c–e), and of course the very end of the dialogue describes Socrates growing cold as he dies (118a). Finally, and most important, if one generalizes the point that Crito makes, it is of some interest. Talking staves off death; that is, conversation, dialectic, *dialegesthai*, talking to someone makes you live longer. The more Socrates talks the harder it will be to kill him, the closer he will get to immortality, to overcoming the problem of death. We must try to understand what this might mean.

The suggestion is that conversation provides a sort of substitute for death. This would mean that it serves the function that death serves; it would then provide a sort of detachment of the self from the interests of the self. We cannot begin to argue this now, but it

25 *Nietzsche* II, 953.

does have a certain *prima facie* plausibility. We speak of conversations having a life of their own; they are not simply under the control of the conversants. They are, so to speak, disembodied. What is true of conversation is also to some extent true of conversations with ourselves – our thoughts. Thinking is a kind of speech, a *logos*, that the soul has with itself. Later on, in what is certainly the most famous part of the *Phaedo*, Socrates provides his listeners with an intellectual autobiography. In the course of his account of himself, Socrates says that he discovered the impossibility of philosophizing by looking directly at beings; in looking directly, one ran the risk of being blinded as one does who looks directly at the sun during an eclipse. Instead, Socrates began to examine things through their images in speeches – in *logoi*. He refers to this as a second sailing, a second-best way, made necessary by the impossibility of the best way, an immediate apprehension of the being of things. I suggest that the necessity to look for a second-best way is the same as the necessity for finding an alternative to death. In both instances Socrates turns to speeches – to *logoi*.

That the solution to the problem of human mortality comes in some mediated way through the *logos* has an interesting irony. The common sense solution to the problem of mortality was immortality, an immortality that transformed itself into a death wish. There is a commonsensical level to the claim that immortality comes through speeches as well. Socrates achieves a sort of immortality by being remembered, and he is remembered through his speeches. The *Phaedo* is constructed with this in mind. This immortality is of course spurious. But what lies behind it is not. The speeches and Socrates are memorable precisely because of the extraordinary level of detachment which they display.

Finally, that his is the direction in which one must seek Plato's solution to the problem of mortality is clear from one other piece of evidence. Phaedo narrates that as Socrates' friends were entering his cell for the last time his wife Xanthippe was leaving. When she saw them she cried out "O, Socrates, this is the last time your comrades will address you and you them" (60a). Socrates has her sent home. I believe Xanthippe puts her finger on what is for Socrates the truly sad part of his death. Whatever access human beings have to immortality would seem to be a peculiarly mortal immortality. While this is not nihilism, neither is it perfect. As usual, the last word belongs to Xanthippe.

Chapter 10

THE EMPIRE OF POETRY: ON SHAKESPEARE'S *TITUS ANDRONICUS*[1]

In the Shakespeare wars the battle over *Titus Andronicus* is ongoing. According to one camp Shakespeare did not write the play – or at least he didn't write all of it. For others he wrote it – but it is his worst play.[2] Now, in this latter group, some still "defend" it. According to Frank Kermode, while "nobody has ever called Titus anything but the least of Shakespeare's tragedies," still it is "unjustly despised."[3] And, again speaking for the defense, Russ McDonald: "Shakespeare's first tragedy is clearly the effort of an ambitious and unpublished playwright."[4] Others are less kind. An early adaptor of the play (1678) calls *Titus* "rather a heap of rubbish than a structure"[5] For T.S. Eliot it is "one of the stupidest and most uninspired

1 Originally given as the inaugural lecture in the Sara Yates Exley Lecture Series in the Great Books, Sarah Lawrence College, spring 2004.
2 For a discussion of the authenticity of the play see *The Yale Shakespeare: The Complete Works*, Cross, W.L. and Brooke, T., eds. (New York: Barnes and Noble, 1993), 857-61.
3 *The Riverside Shakespeare* (Boston: Houghton Mifflin, 1974), 1019.
4 Introduction to *Titus Andronicus*, The Pelican Shakespeare (New York: Penguin Books Inc., 2000), xxix.
5 Ravenscroft, Edward in his Preface to his 1687 revision of the play, quoted in

plays ever written," and for Tennessee Williams "one of the most ridiculous."[6] Now, that said, on the principle that even on a bad day, Shakespeare is generally better than anyone else, perhaps *Titus Andronicus* is worth a second look.

Where there is so much smoke surely there is some fire; so why is *Titus Andronicus* held in such contempt? There are generally two sorts of objections to it. On the one hand, it is thought excessively violent. It begins with human sacrifice and ends with Titus feeding Tamora, queen of the Goths, her children. In between there is rape and the severing of hands, heads, and tongue. Understandably this makes good people a little squeamish. On the other hand, there is the poetry of the play, which seems to range from too flat to too florid. McDonald points to its "thumpingly regular iambic pentameter"[7] – *Titus* has only one brief part of a scene in prose (IV.3). And then there is its merciless deployment of the "lowest form of humor" – the pun; we have "more" and "Moor"; "dear," and "deer"; "wit," "whit," and "white"; "Horace" and "whore-ass"; "goat" and "Goth"; "mark" and "Marcus"; "right," "rite," and "write," and so on. But perhaps most striking is its unprecedented number of poetic and literary references, making it seem uncharacteristically derivative even for Shakespeare. There are at least twenty-seven references to Ovid (primarily to the *Metamorphoses*), seven to Vergil, six to Livy, several to Horace and Seneca, as well as references to Cicero, Herodotus, Plutarch, Sophocles, Aeschylus, Euripides, Homer and Chaucer – not to mention the possible self-references to Shakespeare's *The Rape of Lucrece* – written at about the same time as *Titus*. This is a play that seems to require footnotes (perhaps Eliot should have liked it better). Now, when a poet of Shakespeare's caliber writes a play in which two unconnected things seem so disproportionately prominent, it is usually worth asking whether the two are so disconnected as we first take them to be. Our puzzle then? Is there a connection between poetry and violence?

The Yale Shakespeare: The Complete Works, Cross, W.L. and Brooke, T. , eds. (New York: Barnes and Noble, 1993), 857.

6 Quoted by McDonald, Introduction to *Titus Andronicus*, xxx.

7 Introduction to *Titus Andronicus*, xl.

I: Violence

Let's sidle up to the issue of violence by asking some provisional questions. Where is this play set? *Titus Andronicus* is emphatically in Rome – "Rome" and "Romans" occur sixty-eight times in Act I – more than in the rest of the play combined.[8] But which Rome – i.e., when? All of the characters in the play are fictional. There is no historical Titus Andronicus; the closest approximation seems to be Lucius Livius Andronicus – a poet who introduces drama to Rome in about 240 B.C. Tamora seems to be based on Herodotus' account of Tomyris – queen of the Massegetae in about 550 B.C.[9] There was briefly an "emperor" Saturninus – he was one of nineteen pretenders to the imperial throne (called the "thirty tyrants") after the death of Valerian in about 260 A.D. *Titus* begins with the return of the army to Rome after victory in the war with the Goths. There were wars with the Goths on and off after 235 A.D., and the Goths were defeated, on and off, until about 270 A.D., after which there is a hiatus in the wars for about a hundred years. So, what evidence there is seems to point to 260 A.D. as the historical time in which Shakespeare has set his play. This fits with the fact that *Titus Andronicus* is clearly set in imperial Rome, although the Rome of the play is one in which the tribunes and senate wield considerably more power than they did in the real Rome of 260 A.D. This date also fits with the three Christian references in the play.[10] Constantine begins the gradual official introduction of Christianity into the empire in 312 A.D.; obviously it was already in the air in 260. In a way, then, the play can be dated, but in another way it seems to span the whole history of Rome – republican, imperial, and Christian.

The first scene opens with a crisis of succession. The old emperor, who is never named, is dead. There seem at first two possible successors – Saturninus and his younger brother Bassianus, sons of the emperor. Saturninus indicates the principle of his claim in the

8   In Act II there are six references to Rome and Romans, in Act III ten, in Act IV 20, and in Act V 23.
9   Herodotus, *History* I.201–16.
10 "Holy water" occurs at I.1.326, "St. Stephen" at IV.4.43, and "popish tricks" at V.1.76.

play's very first line: "Noble *pat*ricians, *pat*rons of my right" (italics mine). His appeal is based on his paternity and his status as the eldest son. Bassianus, on the other hand, bases his claim on his virtue – his natural superiority. He addresses his supporters as "Romans, friends, followers" (I.1.9) and calls for a "pure election" in which Romans will exercise "freedom in their choice" (I.1.16–17). Two principles of succession are at odds here, one having to do with heredity, family, and hierarchy and the other with election, virtue, and equality. This is where things stand until the tribune Marcus Andronicus enters and offers his brother Titus – a hardened general and newly returned from his victories in the Gothic War – as a third candidate. In one fell swoop, the other two are also-rans.

Yet Titus's claim diminishes Bassianus much more than it does Saturninus, for Titus is proposed by a tribune who claims to stand "for the people of Rome" (I.1.20), and Titus's record of service to Rome is unrivaled. Titus therefore has the greater claim to be the candidate of the democratic faction. That is, Bassianus's position is shown to be self-contradicting. To oppose his brother he must appeal to the democratic principle and to his superior virtue, but so superior is Titus on both counts, that were he not the emperor's son, Bassianus wouldn't even be in the running.

During this scene we learn several details about Titus soon to become very relevant. He has made enormous family sacrifices for Rome. He has been away for ten years fighting a war in which twenty-one of his twenty-five sons have died – the number will soon be twenty-two. It is perhaps worth noting that there is never any mention of the mother of these sons. Titus is surnamed Pius. He is no democrat – it is his (younger?) brother Marcus who puts forward his claim.

Now, in what seems a failure of judgment worthy of King Lear, Titus Andronicus throws his support to Saturninus. The only reason explicitly given by Titus is that Saturninus is eldest (I.1.227). For Titus, apparently, there is no difference between the principle of virtue and the principle of heredity. Although Saturninus, who shows himself rather villainous, has just threatened civil war to get his way (I.1.208), Titus predicts that under his rule "his virtues will . . . reflect on Rome Titan's rays on earth and ripen justice in this commonweal" (I.1.28–30).

All of this has to do with Titus's curious, but consistent, conflation of the familial and the political. For him, the difference between Rome and the Andronici is very difficult to make out, as the following passages taken together make clear:[11]

> Romans, of five and twenty valiant sons,
> Half of the number that King Priam had,
> Behold the poor remains, alive and dead.
> (Titus at I.1.82–84)

> Titus, unkind and careless of thine own,
> Why suffer'st thou thy sons unburied yet,
> To hover on the dreadful shore of Styx?
> Make way to lay them by their brethren.
> (Titus at I.1.89–92)

> Give us the proudest prisoner of the Goths,
> That we may hew his limbs and on a pile
> *Ad manes fratrum* [to the spirits of our brothers] sacrifice his flesh
> Before this earthly prison of their bones
> That so the shadows be not unappeased,
> Nor we disturbed with prodigies on earth.
> (Lucius – Titus's eldest son – at I.1.99–104)

> Patient yourself, madam, and pardon me.
> These are their brethren whom your Goths beheld
> Alive and dead, and for their brethren slain
> Religiously they ask a sacrifice.
> To this your son is marked, and dies he must,
> T'appease their groaning shadows that are gone.
> (Titus to Tamora at I.1.124–29)

> See, lord and father, how we have performed
> Our Roman rites. Alarbus's limbs are lopped
> And entrails feed the sacrificing fire,
> Whose smoke like incense doth perfume the sky
> Remaineth naught but to inter our brethren

---

11 See also I.1.18–26, 174, 256, 352–57, 425.

And with loud 'larums welcome them to Rome.
(Lucius at I.1.145–50)

Titus Andronicus, then, would seem to be the *perfect* citizen who makes no distinction whatsoever between the good of Rome and the good of his family – of his own. The principle of Roman justice may be *suum cuique* – "to each his own" (I.1.283) – but for Titus Andronicus, Rome is identical to his own. His actions on its behalf are so sure as to be automatic. Accordingly, Marcus can say with utter confidence that Titus has "this day" "done sacrifice" and slain the "noblest prisoner of the Goths" (I.1.35–38) a hundred lines before the sacrifice is actually completed. Apparently you can always count on Titus Andronicus to do the right/rite thing. Titus's conflation of his family with Rome is unquestioned. After he accepts Saturninus's offer to wed his daughter Lavinia, Bassianus claims that she is already betrothed to him and so flees with her. When his son Mutius tries to stop Titus from following the two, he kills him without a second thought. Titus does this not because the boy tried to thwart his father but with these words: "What, villain boy? Barr'st me my way in *Rome?*" (I.1.293–94, italics mine). Titus then refuses to bury Mutius's corpse in the family tomb with the following words:

Traitors, away. He rests not in this tomb:
This monument five hundred years hath stood,
Which I have sumptuously redefined.
Here none but soldiers and Rome's servitors
Repose in fame; none basely slain in brawls.
Bury him where you can, he comes not here.
(I.1.352–57)

The Andronici line, then, goes back to about 240 B.C.

In the first scene, then, without batting an eye, Titus Andronicus performs human sacrifice (there is no historical record that such a rite ever existed in Rome), kills his son and refuses him burial, and makes an unjust and brutal man emperor. In all three instances, the reason for his action is his unquestioned loyalty to Rome, which he understands as indistinguishable from his family. Several things are crucial here. First, all the violence that follows in the play would

have been avoided had Titus granted Tamora's plea to save her son –
a plea that she begins with "Roman brethren!" (I.1.107). Second,
when Titus names Saturninus emperor, it is admittedly for the sake
of preventing civil war in Rome. This problem shows up at the very
beginning of the play as a conflict of brothers – Saturninus versus
Bassianus. There are several similar conflicts in *Titus Andronicus*.
Saturninus and Bassianus also quarrel over Lavinia. And in a way
Titus and Marcus too can be seen to quarrel over Lavinia. When
Titus promises her to Saturninus, Bassianus makes the surprising
claim that she is already betrothed to him. Who betrothed her? Titus
clearly has the authority to make this decision as his immediate
response to Saturninus's offer indicates (I.1.246–48). But Titus, who
has been away for ten years, is clearly in the dark about what
Bassianus, with the support of Lucius and Marcus, says is his lawful claim. Did Marcus, who makes the prior claim of Bassianus a
matter of *his* honor (I.1.480), usurp his brother's authority to decide
whom Lavinia will marry? In general, in *Titus Andronicus*, civil
strife breaks out when brothers quarrel over questions having to do
with women and marriage (this will also prove true of Tamora's
sons, who quarrel over Lavinia). This is of special interest in understanding Titus's relation to Rome, for Rome cannot be a family if it
contains other families. This is why the play can have in it only one
Roman woman, who is in several ways the cause of strife and civil
war. There can be no mothers in Rome (we hear of Titus's 26 children but never of his wife) because Rome is *the* mother – "she
whom mighty kingdoms curtsy to" (V.37.4). Tamora is, of course,
the exception that proves the rule since she is not Roman – she is
"incorporate in Rome." Saturninus must practice exogamy if the
family of Rome is to be kept intact.[12]

So Roman is Titus that he has no alternative principle of right to
which to appeal in order to judge Rome. He is surnamed Pius, and
his religion is the identity of the Andronici and Rome. Tamora is
therefore not wrong when she accuses him of "irreligious piety"
(I.1.133).[13] And her sons are not wrong in calling the Romans "bar-

12 The model for the family in Rome thus seems to be the family of Titus's tomb;
   see I.1.153–59.
13 Here and elsewhere, Titus Andronicus seems the mirror image of Antigone,
   whose pious sin is her devotion to the family. See Sophocles' *Antigone* 74.

barians" (I.1.134–44). The question then is what is responsible for this barbaric metamorphosis of Rome's most perfect citizen, and with him Rome. What makes it possible for Lucius to describe human sacrifice by saying that its "smoke like incense doth perfume the sky" (I.1.148)?

Perhaps we may get a sense of what causes the violence of *Titus Andronicus* by looking at what proves strong enough to overcome this equation of Rome and family. When Titus refuses to bury Mutius in the family tomb, Marcus accuses him of impiety (I.1.358); Titus isn't impressed. Then Marcus and his son Quintus entreat him in the name of the naturalness of the family (I.1.373–74); Titus is unmoved. Finally, Marcus says

> Thou art a Roman, be not barbarous:
> The Greeks upon advice did bury Ajax,
> That slew himself; and wise Laertes' son
> Did graciously plead for his funerals
> Let not young Mutius then, that was thy joy,
> Be barred his entrance here.
> (I.1.381–86)

Titus is finally convinced by way of an appeal to Sophocles' *Ajax* – to poetry. This brings us to the second half of our puzzle – the prominence of poetry and of literary references in *Titus Andronicus*.

II: Poetry

Poetry appears in a double way in *Titus Andronicus*. There are a host of literary references – distributed throughout the play but especially prominent in Acts II and IV. And the play itself, of course, is a poem. On the one hand, it is perhaps more a poem than any other play of Shakespeare – remember the "thumpingly regular iambic pentameter." On the other hand, there are long stretches of the play that are unusually barren of poetic imagery.

Let's begin with the second point – the poetry of the play itself. Titus enters in Act I, scene 1 with a simile in the Homeric style, comparing himself to a ship returning to harbor.

> Hail Rome, victorious in thy mourning weeds!
> Lo, as the bark that hath discharged her fraught
> Returns with precious lading to the bay

> From whence at first she weighed her anchorage,
> Cometh Andronicus, bound with laurel boughs,
> To re-salute his country with his tears,
> Tears of true joy for his return to Rome.
> (I.1.73–79)

Curiously, however, there is nothing else of this sort in Act I. In fact, there is no poetic imagery at all in the rest of Act I. Once Titus is actually in Rome, he essentially speaks prose, however thumpingly regular the verse in which he speaks it. Our attention is called to this by the first speech of Act II, the entry into the play of Aaron the Moor, Tamora's lover and co-conspirator. The speech is an elaborate simile describing Aaron's relation to Tamora; it is worth citing in part.

> Now climbeth Tamora Olympus' top,
> Safe out of fortune's shot, and sits aloft,
> Secure of thunder's crack or lightning flash,
> Advanced above pale envy's threatening reach.
> As when the golden sun salutes the morn,
> And having gilt the ocean with his beams,
> Gallops the zodiac in his glistering coach
> And overlooks the highest-peering hills,
> So Tamora
> Upon her with doth earthly honor wait,
> And virtue stoops and trembles at her frown.
> Then Aaron, arm thy heart and fit thy thoughts
> To mount aloft with thy imperial mistress,
> And mount her pitch whom thou in triumph long
> Hast prisoner held, fettered in chains,
> And faster bound to Aaron's charming eyes
> Than is Prometheus tied to Caucasus.
> (II.1.1–17)

Aaron is an interesting character; he is an expert at conspiracy and deception. So, he conspires with Tamora (who conspires in turn with Saturninus) in the death of Bassianus[14] and in the rape of Lavinia. But Tamora's sons, Demetrius and Chiron, do not know in advance that part of this plot involves the killing of Bassianus. Aaron must

---

14 That Saturninus has knowledge of the plot is clear when one compares II.3.251–52 and 257–58 with 263.

tell Tamora to be cross with Bassianus so as to move her sons to back her in a quarrel (II.3.53–54). Were they in on the plan, this charade would be altogether gratuitous. Neither is Saturninus fully in the know; he does not know that the plot involves the rape of Lavinia and, when he hears of it, seems prepared to punish them (V.3.59). The sons of Tamara, in turn, are ignorant of the fact that Aaron is sleeping with their mother. Aaron, thus, seems to deceive everyone in the play but Tamora, and in the end he deceives her about what he intends to do with their child, the proof of her infidelity to Saturninus that will ruin everything for her. Aaron reveals himself fully to no one in the play. He is the ultimate outsider who never altogether gives himself away until the end, when he agrees to tell all in order to save his child's life. At this point, he gives several long speeches, none of which contain poetic images. Titus, on the other hand, resumes the use of poetry in Rome only after the arrest of his two sons on the charge of murdering Bassianus when he says that "Rome is but a wilderness of tigers" (III.1.54). This resumption marks the beginning of his estrangement from Rome. He becomes an outsider.

One final thing about the poetry in *Titus Andronicus*. There is a good deal of lying in the play, but several times it becomes so elaborate as to become a play within a play, as in the scene preceding the rape of Lavinia by Demetrius and Chiron, where Tamora starts a quarrel with Bassianus and Lavinia so as to give her sons a pretext to intervene. It is true most of all in Act V, where Tamora and her sons impersonate Revenge, Rape, and Murder in an attempt to manipulate a credulous Titus into entrapping his son Lucius – now in command of an army of Goths ready to invade Rome to avenge the death of his brothers, the rape of his sister, and the loss of his father's hand. This is followed by a scene where Titus becomes a servile cook in order to feed Tamora her two sons in a pie. In none of these scenes is the language particularly poetic; nevertheless the fact of the drama is poetic. While they do not *use* images – i.e., language that is not what it is – they themselves are not what they are; they *are* images. As a general rule, then, *Titus Andronicus* is most poetic when characters are not what they are – when they are in one way or another divided against themselves. Presumably to act in a drama and believe in one's role would not be poetic. Rome, then, as it appears in Act I, is a place fully confident in its own worth, where one's humanity is identical to one's being Roman, and where barbarians can be treated as sacrificial animals – i.e., as less than human. This Rome is a place not hospitable to poetry.

If this is so, however, what are we to make of the extraordinary number of poetic and literary references made by Romans in Rome? The dominant reference is to Ovid's *Metamorphoses*, Book VI – to the story of Tereus and Philomela. Aaron first proposes the rape of Lavinia to win Demetrius and Chiron away from their caricature of courtly love in which they are quarrelling over who will be the lover of Lavinia (II.1). He does this by likening Lavinia to Lucrece, whose rape and subsequent suicide was the immediate occasion for the expulsion of the Tarquins, the Roman kings, and the founding of the republic. Demetrius then seals the deal with a quotation from Seneca's *Hippolytus*. Aaron lays out the plan to kill Bassianus and rape Lavinia in terms of the story of Philomela (II.3.43). When the rape is done, Demetrius and Chiron clearly use this story again as a model (although they do not directly cite it) when they cut out Lavinia's tongue and cut off her hands (II.4.1–10). Most peculiar is the scene (IV.1) in which Ovid's *Metamorphoses*, the book itself, becomes a prop in the play. Lavinia is madly following her nephew, the young Lucius, around the house. No one understands the meaning of her behavior. Marcus first interprets this event in terms of an historical reference to the mother of the Gracchi, Cornelia.

> See Lucius, see, how much she makes of thee:
> Some whither would she have thee go with her.
> Ah, boy, Cornelia never with more care
> Read to her sons than she hath read to thee
> Sweet poetry and Tully's *Orator*.
> (IV.1.10–14)

The boy interprets it in terms of another story from Ovid, the story of Hecuba of Troy (IV.1.20). Lavinia then turns to the books that Lucius, in his anxiety, has let fall. Titus misinterprets her behavior. He thinks she wishes to while away the time while waiting for heaven to reveal who raped her, although he is a bit puzzled about why she raises her handless arms to heaven (IV.1.30–37). Marcus then interprets this action ambiguously – either she means that her attackers numbered more than one or else "to heaven she heaves them [her hands] for revenge" (IV.1.40). Then Lavinia turns to the *Metamorphoses*, and Marcus misinterprets this: "For love of her that's gone/ perhaps she culled it from the rest" (IV.143–44) – that is for love of the boy's mother who gave him the book. Lavinia then turns to the story of Philomela; this still doesn't reveal the rapists. The whole thing is developed in this queer way until Lavinia finally reveals who raped her by writing it down in the sand – i.e., by writing and not by reading. The point of the scene seems to be that Lavinia's rape is "understood" so well by all the parties concerned in terms of poetic and historical precedents – Philomela, her tongue cut out by her rapist brother-in-law Tereus, weaves the story of her rape into a tapestry and sends it to her sister – that they are paralyzed. They have Philomela so in mind that they cannot revise what Philomela did so as to do what she did. The whole scene is thus a sort of macabre comedy of errors. They understand the world so thoroughly in terms of the body of literature that forms them that they are no longer in any real contact with the world.

The poetic references of *Titus Andronicus* provide the lens through which the characters of the play see their world. They understand what is *right* only by way of various *rites* and through what the various poets and historians *write*. Titus threatens Aaron in verse by quoting Horace (IV.2.20–21). Even his elaborate revenge at the end is a sort of literary citation. Titus kills his own daughter using as a model a story from Livy in which Virginia, a Roman maid, is killed by her father in order to keep the tyrannical Decemvir Appius Claudius from raping her. Then he avenges himself on Tamora by using as a model Philomela's sister Procne, who "like a tigress" kills her son Itys and serves him to his father Tereus "pretending it was a sacred ritual."[15]

Only once in the play does Shakespeare actually quote Ovid. At the beginning of Act IV, scene 3, Titus announces *Terras Astraea reliquit* – "the goddess Justice has left the earth."[16] This begins a

---

15 Ovid, *Metamorphoses*, VI.600 ff.
16 Ovid, *Metamorphoses*, I.150.

mad scene in which Titus first tells the others to seek for justice in Pluto's realm (i.e., in hell), after which they fire arrows aloft – sending messages to heaven. This is followed by the prose scenelet with a clown; the exchange looks very much like a brief hint about a religion of extremely humble origins that will not recognize Jupiter as a god – i.e., about Christianity. Titus tries to get this humble clown to carry a supplication to Saturninus. Sadly, though the clown will swear by St. Stephen (the first Christian martyr), he cannot deliver his supplication with sufficient grace and is hanged. Titus, then, appeals to every possible power of earth and heaven for justice, but it is in vain. Now, in Ovid, this flight of Justice is at the very beginning of the *Metamorphoses*. It follows directly after Ovid's account of the progressive deterioration of humanity from Gold to Silver to Bronze and finally to the Iron Age, when all manner of crime breaks out. Jupiter looks down from heaven and groans as he remembers the recent dinner of Lycaon, who tried to test the gods by feeding them human flesh and who offered them human sacrifices. Lycaon was changed into a wolf by Jupiter, his new shape perfectly suiting his nature; this is the first metamorphosis in Ovid's book. Ovid then tells us that the gods demanded this punishment and that their dismay was like that felt by human beings when a wicked bond of fanatics tried to extinguish the Roman name by shedding the blood of Caesar; the last metamorphosis of the book is Caesar's – he is changed into a star.

The flight of justice in *Titus Andronicus* is not an accident. The play begins with human sacrifice and ends with cannibalism. And all the violence in between is linked to the strange character of Rome. In Rome the emperor is a god (IV.4.82). Accordingly, there can be no appeal to anything beyond Rome. The good Roman is thus identical to the good man – there is no remainder. There is therefore no poetry in Rome because Rome is so thoroughly poetic as to obscure the reality that might give rise to poetry. It is like Plato's cave, but with the entrance sealed and so with no access to the natural light of the sun by which one might know the shadows on the wall to be mere shadows. No one makes poetry in Titus's Rome; there is only that mixture of poetry and tradition that Romans quote and do not distinguish from the real. It is not uninteresting, then, that according to the Greek version of Ovid's story, Philomela and Procne become birds, while in Latin *philomela* comes to mean "nightingale" and *procne*, "swallow." In Rome, things are what they mean. One might say that Rome is a metaphor that, because it does not know itself to be a metaphor, admits no Homeric simile. At first this looks to be perfect justice, but in fact it leads to complete barbarism, for in the end nothing remains to temper righteousness.

At first, Titus Andronicus seems to have learned this when he recognizes that Rome has become "a wilderness of tigers" (III.1.54). But by the end a curious reversal has occurred. The consequence of Titus's carefully scripted revenge is that his son, Lucius Andronicus, becomes emperor. And Lucius is perhaps the least poetic character in the play. Now, Lucius is not actually elected emperor – republican forms have apparently seen their last days. Instead, he is simply declared to be the choice of the "common voice" (V.3.140). Lucius's first act as emperor is to mete out punishment, first to Aaron:

> Set him breast-deep in earth, and famish him.
> There let him stand and rave and cry for food.
> If anyone relieves or pities him,
> For the offense, he dies. This is our doom.
> Some stay to see him fastened in the earth.
> (V.3.179–83)

and then to the corpse of Tamora:

> As for that ravenous tiger, Tamora,
> No funeral rite, nor man in mourning weeds,
> No mournful bell shall ring her burial,
> But throw her forth to beasts and birds to prey.
> Her life was beastly and devoid of pity,
> And being dead, let birds on her take pity!
> (V.3.195–200)

This is a fate often threatened in the *Iliad* but never meted out. If the lines printed in the second Quarto (but not in the first) truly belong to the play, *Titus Andronicus* would end with these words.

> See justice done on Aaron, that damned Moor,
> By whom our heavy haps had their beginning.

> Then, afterwards, to order well the state,
> That like events may ne'er it ruinate.
> (V.3.201–4)

The result of Titus Andronicus's restoration of Rome is thus the ascension of an emperor particularly barbaric because he upholds civilization with utter self-confidence and not a whit of self-restraint. That Lucius should come to power at the end of the play is especially significant when one remembers that the dramatic date of this play is about 260 A.D., and Titus places the age of his family tomb at 500 years. His family thus dates from about 240 B.C. – i.e., from the time of the poet Lucius Livius Andronicus, who first introduced dramatic poetry to Rome. *Titus Andronicus* is therefore the story of how Lucius Livius Andronicus finally becomes the emperor of Rome. It takes 500 years, but, in the end, dramatic poetry so completely conquers Rome as to turn it altogether barbaric. The empire of poetry means that there is no poetry in Rome because Rome is a poem.

In *Titus Andronicus*, Shakespeare has therefore written a play in which he warns us of the danger of a poetry – and specifically of a dramatic poetry – that becomes so powerful as to replace the reality it is initially meant to render. And when reality no longer constrains, human beings will stop at nothing in pursuit of their ends. This, of course, does describe the barbarians in the play – Tamora and her sons and Aaron. Yet the true tragedy of *Titus Andronicus* is that in the end it is Titus himself who will stop at nothing in the pursuit of the holy, and Titus is meant to represent for us the metamorphosis of Rome. It is therefore perhaps not accidental that as Shakespeare has Touchstone tell us in *As You Like It* (III.3.5–6) in a pun on goats, Ovid was exiled among the Goths, who, he writes in *Tristia* V.10.37, thought he was a barbarian.

Chapter 11

AGREEING TO AGREE:
ON BEGINNING ROUSSEAU'S
SOCIAL CONTRACT[1]

By general agreement, Rousseau stands out as a great champion
of the natural equality of men. Though we may be everywhere in
chains, we are born free; this is the foundation of our equality.
Accordingly, Rousseau also seems to champion a kind of pure par-
ticipatory democracy, a government that can originate legitimately
only in a universal agreement among those who are to be governed
by it. He calls this unanimity the General Will; when it speaks, it is
sovereign. This authority, constituted by all of us to rule all of us, is
the mark of our civil and moral freedom. It all seems so simple and
congenial to contemporary tastes that it is at first a little disturbing
to discover that it is quite impossible. What I would like to do this
afternoon is turn to the beginning of Rousseau's *Of the Social
Contract* to see why.

It was Rousseau's habit to place epigraphs at the beginning of his
writings. At first blush, the passages quoted seem harmless enough.
Yet, without exception, they are oddly inappropriate. Why, for example, is a quotation from Aristotle's justification for natural slavery in
the *Politics* placed at the head of an argument designed to establish

1 Presented in the Humanities Colloquium Lecture Series, Sarah Lawrence
College, Spring 1996.

that human beings are by nature equal (*Discourse on the Origin and Foundations of Inequality Among Men*)? And, isn't it queer that a quotation from Ovid (*Tristia*) should be the epigraph for a book in which Ovid is numbered with Catullus and Martial as "among that crowd of obscene authors whose names alone alarm decency?"[2] In a defense of this book, the *Discourse on the Sciences and the Arts*, Rousseau wrote the following:

> Some precautions were, at first, necessary, and it is in order to make everything understood that I did not want to say everything. It is only successively and only for a few readers that I have developed my ideas. It was not myself that I spared but the truth, so as to make it pass more surely and render it useful. Often I was at great pains to try to conceal in a sentence, in a line, in a word tossed off as if by chance the result of a long series of reflections. Often the greater part of my readers must have found my discourses badly connected and nearly entirely disjointed for want of perceiving the trunk of which I showed them only the branches. But that was enough for those who knew how to understand, and I have never wanted to speak to the others.[3]

That Rousseau plies this same art of writing in *Of the Social Contract* is clear from a note in his *Judgment on the Polysynod of the Abbé de Saint-Pierre.*

> I would wager that here again a thousand people will find a contradiction with the Social Contract. That proves that there are still more readers who ought to learn to read than authors who ought to learn to be consistent.[4]

Rousseau seems to go out of his way to warn us that we take him at face value at our own peril.

Now, *Of the Social Contract* begins with an epigraph taken from Book 11 of Virgil's *Aeneid* – "In an equitable federation, let us make

2 *Discourse on the Sciences and Arts*, paragraph 20.
3 "Préface d'une seconde lettre . . . Bordes," paragraph 9. The translation is my own.
4 *Oeuvre Complêtes*, p. 364. My attention was first called to this passage by Roger Masters's Introduction to his *The First and Second Discourses* (New York: St. Martin's, 1964), 26.

laws." It seems meant to indicate that the founding of the Roman republic, once hailed by Rousseau as "that model of all free peoples," is a paradigm for the social contract.[5] The context in the *Aeneid* makes this claim rather peculiar, however. Aeneas has led the Trojans who survived the war with the Greeks to Italy where they offer to live peacefully with the Latins, whose king, Latinus, wants to offer his daughter, Lavinia, in marriage to Aeneas. Turnus, the greatest warrior among the Latins, objects – Lavinia had been promised to him. There are lots of complications, but the upshot is that the hawks among the Latins triumph, and Turnus leads them into a war with the Trojans, which at the moment (in Book XI) is going rather badly for them. Upon hearing that Diomedes, the Greek from whom they had requested support, has refused them (he has had enough of war and has nothing against the Trojans) Latinus, who has been a dove all along, makes a speech in which he proposes peace with the Trojans – "in an equitable federation, let us make laws." The meeting breaks up without settling anything because the Trojans are at the gates. In the renewed fighting Aeneas kills Turnus, and the Latins are about to be defeated. We do not see the immediate results, but presumably Aeneas conquers and dictates terms.

Now, how is this a paradigm for a social contract – a peaceful agreement of free and equal men? However peaceful the first intentions of the parties involved, as presented here, the founding of Rome results from an act of force. There is further difficulty (or perhaps it is the same). Why does Rousseau choose as an epigraph an allusion to a fictional founding – a poetic legitimation of Rome after the fact? Rousseau, who is known to have chosen his epigraphs with great care and to have considered them to symbolize an entire work, uses this one to cite as a paradigm a "founding" that is fictional, retrospective and the result of an act of force.[6] Are these essential characteristics of the social contract?

One more warning: *Of the Social Contract* begins with a short foreword – an "Avertissement" (five pages later he uses this word in another of its senses, "warning," in a description of declarations of

---

5 See "Letter to Geneva," paragraph 6.
6 *Rousseau Juge de Jean-Jacques*, Dialogue III.

war[7]) – in which Rousseau tells us that it was originally part of a larger project. He destroyed the rest because it proved beyond his powers – his forces – to complete it. Like the social contract, Rousseau's book, *Of the Social Contract*, seems to be an acknowledgment of insufficient force. This is the first of many indications that Rousseau's book is meant on some level to be an example of what he is describing in his book. All right then, what is it that he is describing?

Before we try to penetrate to the trunk of the beginning of Rousseau's argument, perhaps we ought to take a look at a few of its branches. Very roughly, the *Of the Social Contract* divides in two. In the first two books Rousseau traces the origin of political life in the agreement that establishes a sovereign and then articulates the nature and limits of sovereignty. The second part, books three and four, is an account of the origin, powers and limits of government as an instrument of this sovereign.

Sovereignty is thus central to Rousseau's argument. Without it there is no social order. Where then does it originate? Rousseau first tries to discredit the competition. He argues that society is not natural (as it is for example in Aristotle); it originates neither in the family (I.2.¶'s 1–3) nor in some natural inequality justifying slavery (I.2. ¶'s 4–9). Nor can it originate in conquest or force (I.3) for right has nothing to do with force.

> Yielding to force is an act of necessity, not of will. At most, it is an act of prudence. In what sense could it be a duty? . . . If it is necessary to obey by force, one need not obey by duty, and if one is no longer forced to obey, one is no longer obligated to do so. It is apparent, then, that this word right adds nothing to force. It is meaningless here. . . . Obey those in power. If that means yield to force, the precept is good, but superfluous; I reply that it will never be violated. (I.3. ¶'s 2–3)

Sovereignty can also not originate in an agreement to become a slave (I.4) – this is Rousseau's understanding of Hobbes – for no

---

7   *Of the Social Contract*, Book 1, chapter 4, paragraph 11.

such agreement is possible. One can of course be a slave, but one can never consistently agree to be a slave, for such an agreement would be a tacit declaration of independence. One enters into an agreement for some benefit, but there can be no benefits for a being who has given up his right to have any independent interests. Accordingly, Rousseau argues, sovereignty must be traceable to a unanimous agreement of the members of a society – whether explicit or tacit – and, since in an agreement the parties meet as equals and are equally bound, all society presupposes a fundamental equality of those who make it up.

Now, no doubt Rousseau is in some sense serious about this argument; still, he knows it is harder than he has made it seem. Consider, for example, the most famous lines of the book:

> Man was/is born free, and everywhere he is in chains. . . . How did this change occur? I do not know. What can make it legitimate? I believe I can answer this question.
> (I.1. ¶ 1)

Did I get this right? Does the great champion of natural equality identify the subject matter of the *Of the Social Contract* as legitimate slavery?

Or, consider the family. Rousseau, who says that he was "born a citizen of a free state" (I. ¶3), also says that

> the family is therefore, so to speak [*si l'on veux* or literally: if one wills it], the first model of political societies. The leader is the image of the father, the people are the image of the children; and since all are born equal and free, they only alienate their freedom for their utility. (I.2. ¶3)

Of course, we no more choose our families than Rousseau chose to be born a citizen of Geneva. We may voluntarily alienate our freedom only when we are old enough to have it, but by the time we reach the "age of reason" at which we are capable of judging the proper means of determining our own preservation, we have long since become accustomed to the inequalities of family life. The social contract, our agreement to be ruled, occasions so little fanfare as to pass by altogether unnoticed. This is beautifully expressed by Rousseau's use of the idiom *si l'on veux*. The family is a model of political society only if one wills it, but this willing, like an idiom, is so taken for granted as to mask its own presence.

The same point is made somewhat differently in Rousseau's discussion of slavery.

> Aristotle was right, but he mistook the effect for the cause. Every man born in slavery is born for slavery; nothing could be more certain. Slaves lose everything in their chains, even the desire to be rid of them. They love their servitude as the companions of Ulysses loved their brutishness. If there are slaves by nature, therefore, it is because there have been slaves contrary to nature. Force made the first slaves; their cowardice perpetuated them. (I.2. ¶9)

Even when men think they are slaves (or brutes) they are demonstrating their humanity and not their servility or bestiality. At some level – here, their cowardice – they must agree to their servitude. Apart from its inflammatory rhetoric, what this seems to mean is that force gives way to tacit agreement. Accordingly,

> what man loses by the social contract is his natural freedom and an unlimited right to everything that tempts him and that he can get; what he gains is civil freedom and the proprietorship of everything he possesses. In order not to be mistaken about these compensations, one must distinguish carefully between natural freedom, which is limited only by the force of the individual, and civil freedom, which is limited by the general will; and between possession which is only the effect of force or the right of the first occupant, and property which can only be based on a positive title. (I.8. ¶2)

The social contract gives us "proprietorship in everything we possess," but possession is "only the effect of force." Once again civil society reveals itself to be the legitimation of force. Rousseau begins *Of the Social Contract* with an allusion to a fictional founding because the agreement that originates political life is something of a fiction. On the one hand it cannot really have taken place. And on the other, insofar as it did take place, it is an agreement that presupposes force – an equality that assumes a prior inequality.

Try to imagine for a moment what it would mean for even a small group of people to agree that

> each of us puts his person and all his power in common under the supreme direction of the general will; and we receive each member as an indivisible part of the whole. (I.6. ¶9)

How would such a process begin? Who would make the first move? Does one person place this motion on the table, and then the rest vote? But then hasn't the author of the proposal assumed a position of authority? Hasn't an inequality crept in? And doesn't the very act of voting already imply a willingness to abide by the outcome? That is, doesn't it already imply a prior agreement about the significance of agreement? Every explicit social contract seems to presuppose a prior implicit contract. Rousseau acknowledges as much.

> So that although they [the clauses of this contract] may never have been formally pronounced, they are everywhere the same, everywhere tacitly accepted and recognized. . . . (I.6. ¶5)

If an implicit agreement means an agreement not yet acknowledged, on the explicit level original societies must have come to be from some immediate cause other than agreement. Human beings came together in one way and only later discovered the true significance of their having come together.

One cannot overstate the degree to which this fact dominates the argument of *Of the Social Contract*. It emerges particularly clearly in Rousseau's account of the relation between sovereignty and government. He is at great pains to show that government is only the instrument for executing the general will; it is the means whereby the people as sovereign give laws to themselves as subjects. What we call its laws are in fact only decrees; they are legitimate only to the extent that it is legitimate, and it is legitimized only by the unanimous agreement of the social contract which called it forth. Should the government violate the will of the sovereign constituted by this agreement, it would cease to be a legitimate. Accordingly, the sovereign periodically asks two questions.

> The first: *If it pleases the sovereign to preserve the present form of government.*

The second: *If it pleases the people to leave the administration
to those who are at present in charge.*
(III.18. ¶'s 7–8)

But how does the sovereign go about asking these questions without
an instrument to make its voice heard? Granted that we have peri-
odic elections to determine the will of the people, these elections
must be administered by a government. And if one wants to contest
the results, one goes to court – an arm of government. It is, therefore, strictly speaking, impossible that the sovereign either institute
or dismiss a government without a vehicle for the expression of its
will – a government.

There is no political life without sovereign authority. But genuine sovereignty presupposes a universal consent that is either tacit
– a retroactive affirmation of what has previously existed in the
absence of agreement (i.e., by force) – or else the consent is explicit. But this requires a means for expressing consent – a vehicle that
can only be a government, so that the act of establishing a government to serve as the voice of the sovereign presupposes another government on a more fundamental level, which government would
then be of questionable legitimacy for it could never be authorized
by the sovereign without assuming a still more primordial government. The agreement to agree is impossible. Sovereignty, and with
it political life, rests on a fiction.

The opposition of private or individual interests makes society
necessary. We long for a fair judge of the disputes that inevitably
arise among us. Such responsibility cannot be vested in a single
human being, to be a human being means to have an interest of one's
own – what Rousseau calls an individual will. The first two books
of *Of the Social Contract* point to the sovereign as a general will that
can serve as such a judge because it has, and can have, no individual will or interest *vis-à-vis* its members. As a pure will, it serves,
rather like God, as a pure judge that can be trusted never to substitute its own interest for the interest of those whom it judges. For a
government to be legitimate means for it to bow down before this
authority – to acknowledge that it is not master, but servant. The dif-

ficulty, as we have seen, is that while this authority may be an implication of political life, this does not make it by itself a force than can
initiate or alter political life. What would the law be without its long
arm?

We have a dilemma. There is no government apart from the sovereign of which it is the mere instrument, and there is no sovereign
apart from government without which it can never appear. At the
same time, the government must always defer to the sovereign. How
can this possibly work? Now, while we have only barely scratched
the surface of *Of the Social Contract*, the outlines of Rousseau's
solution are beginning to emerge. What is required for political life
is not so much the existence of the sovereign as the myth of the sovereign as pure servant – a man-made god. The belief in the distinction between government and sovereign would suffice to make
members of the government act as servants and not masters. The
belief in the sovereign is, in a way, sovereign.

Rousseau's *Of the Social Contract* is therefore meant as a moral
education for the social contract. It has two levels. On one level it
assumes the possibility of governmental institutions that assure the
legitimacy of government by checking the tendency for it to devel-
op an interest – an individual will – of its own. Accordingly,
Rousseau gives accounts of how voting should take place, of the
Roman tribunate as an institution within the state that, while it can
do nothing, can prevent everything and is thus "sacred and revered"
as "the preserver of the laws and of legislative power" (IV.5. ¶'s
2–3), of Roman dictatorship as the occasional suspension of the
"sacred power of the laws," a "very necessary providence to realize
that one cannot foresee everything" (IV.6. ¶'s 1–3), and of the office
of Censor as a way of regulating mores, and so laws. In each of these
cases, acknowledging that the state is born from the desire for an
impartial judge but that to perform this function it must employ
men, who are never impartial, Rousseau elaborates political institutions designed to be transpolitical judges of the state.

Yet Rousseau knows that all such institutions must ultimately
prove inadequate. However special, a special prosecutor is still a

prosecutor. "We the people" may amend the constitution, but only through our elected representatives, whether on the federal or state level. All the institutions Rousseau describes point to the divine as the ultimate realization of political life, however problematic this may be. It is no accident that *Of the Social Contract* ends with a long account of civil religion as providing a necessary transpolitical foundation for law. On another level, then, institutions like special prosecutors are not so much meant really to transcend the political as to be constant reminders of the subordination of government to the sovereign. *Of the Social Contract*, therefore, not only teaches us that moral education is the only way to establish a sovereign; it is also an attempt in its own right to establish sovereignty by articulating the myth of the people as sovereign. In the *Aeneid*, Virgil means to affect what Rome is by articulating a new myth of how Rome came to be. Rousseau's *Of the Social Contract* similarly articulates a retroactive founding myth of which we are the heirs.

Chapter 12

UNRAVELING RAVELSTEIN:
SAUL BELLOW'S COMIC TRAGEDY[1]

Ravelstein begins with the word "odd"; it introduces a reflection on the amusing character of the benefactors of mankind. If this beginning is, as advertised, a "clever or wicked footnote" (2), its clever wickedness surely must consist in making us think of Abe Ravelstein as an exemplar of this oddity.[2] A page later the narrator of the novel, Chick, says of the man he is memorializing, "Ravelstein was one of those large men – large, not stout" (3). This proves to be Ravelstein's *leitmotiv*. "He was very tall" (4) (compared especially to his father who was a "fat neurotic little man" – (17). Ravelstein, a "tall pin- or chalk-striped dude with his bald head" (19) was "as big as any of [Michael Jackson's] body guards" (28). "This large Jewish man from Dayton" (94) was "a much larger and graver person" than Rameau's nephew (35). "Ravelstein's extended body was very large, he was nearly six and a half feet tall and his gown, which reached to the ankles of ordinary patients, ended just above his knees" (178). So Ravelstein is larger than life – and larger than Chick.

---

1 Originally part of a roundtable discussion on *Ravelstein* at the 2001 Meeting of the American Political Science Association and later published in *Perspectives on Poitical Science*, Winter 2003, Vol. 32, No.1, 26-31.

2 Parenthetical page numbers refer to Bellow, Saul, *Ravelstein*, (New York: Viking Press, 2000).

> Ravelstein was a bigger man than me. He was able to make a
> striking statement. Because of his larger size, he could wear
> clothes with more dramatic effect. I wouldn't have dreamed of
> disputing this. To be really handsome a man should be tall. A
> tragic hero has to be above the average in height. I hadn't read
> Aristotle in ages but I remembered this much from the *Poetics*.
> (30)

Chick, of course, gets it wrong; it is not the tragic hero of the *Poetics*
who must be tall; rather, the greatness of the great-souled man of the
Nicomachean Ethics is explained by way of a likeness to the bodily
greatness of those who are beautiful, "for the small are urbane and
well proportioned, but not beautiful."[3] Yet perhaps Bellow does not
get it wrong and means to suggest not only that Ravelstein will be a
tragic figure, but also that his tragedy has something to do with
megalopsuchia – greatness of soul or pride. That Ravelstein *is* meant
to be a tragic figure is confirmed by another odd detail – "the
strange shapes of his mismatched feet. One was three sizes bigger
than the other" (18). This is Ravelstein as swell-foot – *Oidi-pous*.
Bellow's novel thus begins by calling our attention to the simultaneously comic and tragic character of Abe Ravelstein. "You don't easily give a creature like Ravelstein to death" (233) for two reasons.
Writing him up is clearly a celebratory act of love; at the same time,
it makes visible a flaw so deep as to be paradigmatic of our humanity. Ravelstein is a big attractive man with a big flaw. To understand
the novel would be to unravel his comic tragedy.

Twice we are told by Chick that he will approach Ravelstein
piecemeal (16, 37), and at first glance he seems as good as his word.
His sketch seems to be a relatively unstructured series of loosely
related impressions – Ravelstein in pieces. But by calling the last
and shortest (214–33) of the novel's four divisions "one more brief
vision," Chick suggests that each of the other three (1–93, 94–159,
160–213) is meant to be taken as a unified vision with internal
coherence. Ravelstein is a man of very specific pieces – pieces
determined by his dominant loves – fine things, friends, and wisdom.

3 Aristotle, *Nicomachean Ethics* 1123b6 (the translation is my own).

The unity of the first section of the novel is thus not surprisingly Ravelstein as the "grandee in the new order of things" (29). He is the proud owner of a $20,000 watch and Lalique crystal; in Paris he stays in the luxury penthouse suite a floor above Michael Jackson at the Crillon and dines at superb restaurants; he throws pizza parties for his students to admire the surpassing excellence of Michael Jordan's game, orders a BMW as a gift for his lover, and possesses an extravagant sound system. Chick is generous with examples; their sum seems designed to convince us of Ravelstein's devotion to the fine – the *kalon*. "These days," says Chick, alluding to one of Aristotle's virtues, "Ravelstein was a magnificent man" (29). The remark calls into question Chick's frequent celebration of his own ignorance of the great books and of the content of Ravelstein's thought. Jerusalem and Athens may not be his dish (15); nevertheless he makes liberal use of Aristotle and of the *Nicomachean Ethics* in particular. Ravelstein's magnificence shows up in his purchase of a $4,500 Lanvin jacket.

> "What does this Lanvin jacket have that your twenty others haven't?" I wanted to say. But I knew perfectly well that in Abe's head there were all kinds of distinctions having to do with prodigality and illiberality, magnanimity and meanness. The attributes of the great-souled man. (32)

Chick shrewdly sees that magnificence (*megaloprepeia*) is simply a preliminary version of greatness of soul (*megalopsuchia*). Both have to do with correctness in estimating worth – the former of things, the latter of oneself. But, as estimating one's own worth requires looking at oneself, willy nilly it means looking at oneself from the outside – as an object of contemplation. Ravelstein's love of fine things is not really separable from his longing to fashion himself into a fine thing. The first part of the novel is thus devoted to Ravelstein's greatness of soul, the virtue Aristotle says consists of being good and knowing it, so as to be able to take pleasure in one's own goodness. This *kosmos* or ornament of all the other virtues manifests itself in autonomy and a contempt for the ordinary. The great-souled man, says Aristotle, "wonders at nothing, for nothing is great to him" (1125a3). (In passing, one might wonder how this affects the stature of philosophy, which according to Aristotle must always originate in wonder.)

The first sentence of the second part of the book seems to point to its unifying principle: "A certain amount of documentation might be offered at this point to show what I was to Ravelstein and Ravelstein to me" (94), and a little later, "We were close friends – what else needs to be added?" (94). Ravelstein is a man devoted to his friends and to the idea of friendship. This second part of the book is filled with possible models for friendship: Chick and his wife Vela ("two solitudes" – 103); Chick and Vela's nominee for a replacement for Ravelstein, Radu Grielescu ("The fact was I enjoyed watching Grielescu. He had so many tics."); Ravelstein and his lover Nikki ("in a special sense, family" – 140); Ravelstein and Morris Herbst ("friends for nearly half a century" who "have so much to say to each other," but "had a few dirty jokes to tell each other first" – 150–51); the Battles, an aging married couple whom Ravelstein talks out of a joint suicide plan; but the friendship between Chick and Ravelstein looms largest – "he and I had become friends – deeply attached – and friendship would not have been possible if we hadn't spontaneously understood each other" (111). This mutual understanding presupposes a certain frankness: "You couldn't, as the intimate and friend of Ravelstein, avoid knowing a great deal more than you had an appetite for" (113), but not confidentiality, for "Ravelstein was crazy about gossip and his friends were given points for the racy items they brought. And it was not a good idea to assume that he would keep the lid on your confidences" (114). The principle of the friendship then is the naked truth (115); nothing is to be off limits. Chick characterizes this complete openness in an odd way:

> . . . it was our sense of what was funny that brought us togeth-
> er, but that would have been a thin anemic way to put it. A joy-
> ful noise – *immenso giubilo* – an outsize joint agreement
> picked us up together, and it would get you nowhere to try to
> formulate it. (118)

The friendship between Chick and Ravelstein is a sort of marriage (Vela actually accuses Chick of having an affair with Ravelstein –

112, and Chick tacitly compares the two by indicating that whereas he and Ravelstein share the sense that everything is potentially funny, Vela finds nothing funny and laughs only when it is conventionally expected – 218). The two are as one in their sense that nothing is too sacred to be looked at, and most of what is held sacred is wonderfully absurd. "As a rule [they spoke] plainly to each other" (125). Ravelstein, for example, is openly critical of Chick's marriage to Vela and of his association with the Grielescus. Because death means "the pictures will stop" and so life is the pictures – the surface of things in which one sees the heart of things (156) – the single thing to be held sacred is fidelity to the true character of the pictures. What Ravelstein so loved in Herbst's late wife Nehamah – "that she was pure and she was immovable" – is a version of what he loves in Chick. That "Nehamah not only refused to see the orthodox rabbi her mother had brought to her deathbed, but never spoke to her again" was a sign for Ravelstein that she was one of "the handful of human beings [who] have the imagination and the qualities of character to live by the true Eros" (144). Chick does not make convenient concessions to the conventional in his thought even when it is hard on others and on himself; this is why Ravelstein enlists him to write him up after he dies: "I want you to show me as you see me, without softeners or sweeteners" (133).

Ravelstein's views of love and friendship are hard to distinguish.

> The marriage of true minds seldom occurs. Love that bears it out even to the edge of doom is not a modern project. But there was, for Ravelstein, nothing to compete with this achievement of the soul. (120)

> [Ravelstein] thought – no, he *saw* – that every soul was looking for its peculiar other, longing for its complement. I'm not going to describe Eros, et cetera, as he saw it. I've done too much of that already: but there is a certain irreducible splendor about it without which we could not be quite human. Love is the highest function of our species – its vocation. This simply can't be set aside in considering Ravelstein. He never forgot this conviction. It figures in all his judgments. (140)

The underlying principle of love here belongs not to Plato but to Plato's Aristophanes; it is love of one's own. But if you are to love your own you must know what really belongs to you; you must know yourself. Accordingly you must seek out another who won't spare you. Ravelstein and Chick share the same sense of what is funny because in principle nothing is excluded from what is funny. Trying to formulate the principle of their attachment would get you nowhere because the principle itself would not be in any sense final or sacred. In principle at least, the two share a fascination with all the pictures – beautiful and ugly.

This is connected to the principle underlying the third part of the novel, a principle at first glance hard to make out. Death is clearly important – this is the part of the book that is most specific about the details of Ravelstein's approaching death and contains as well the account of Chick's near-death experience. It is also the part of the book where their Jewishness is most prominent and where the central importance of Rosamund, Ravelstein's student and Chick's new wife, emerges. But what ties these things together?

Close to the beginning Chick quotes something Rosamund remembers from her school days: "Associate with the noblest people you can find; read the best books; live with the mighty; but learn to be happy alone" (161). Chick more than once protests (not altogether convincingly) that it is his task to describe Ravelstein the person, i.e., not his ideas. Now, to the extent that it is possible to describe a man who, although "he never presented himself as a philosopher," "had had a philosophical training and had learned how a philosophical life should be lived" (173) without speaking of his thought, the object of description would have to be the act of thinking rather than its content. But the act of thinking – of being an observer apart from what is observed and sufficiently neutral to weigh its import – would be, as Aristotle suggests, autonomous. The contemplative life is essentially a life of isolation. Truly to think means to avoid wishful thinking – to look even at what is hardest to bear, the naked truth. Ravelstein accordingly prefers what he calls natural nihilists (Celine, for example) to intellectual nihilists because "they don't tell themselves a lot of high-minded lies" but "accept nihilism as a condition and live in that condition" – they "live with their evils" (175). The evil of evils that we cannot afford to conceal from ourselves is the attempt in the twentieth century to exterminate the Jews. Toward the end Chick reports to Morris Herbst that Ravelstein talked constantly, mostly of Jewish things: "He talked about religion and the difficult project of being man in the fullest sense, of becoming man and nothing but man" (178). Herbst responds "Well, of course he'll keep talking while there's a breath in his body left – and for him it's a top priority, because it's connected with the great evil" (178). These things go together – thinking and the existence of great evil. Chick interprets this to mean that

> the war made it clear that almost everyone agreed that the Jews had no right to live. . . . Other people have some choice of options – their attention is solicited by this issue or that, and being besieged by issues they make their choices according to their inclinations. But for "the chosen" there is no choice. The Jews . . . were historically witnesses to the absence of redemption. (178–79)

Ravelstein reflects on Judaism because to be a Jew at the end of the twentieth century is to have no choice but to live without the illusions engendered by one's inclinations – to acknowledge the ugly. The Jews are permanent outsiders – a solitary people; to reflect on Jewishness then is to reflect on solitude, and solitude is what the contemplative life looks like when it is emptied of ideas. Philosophy as the practice of dying and being dead means neutralizing one's conventional attachments, so as to be able really to look at the world. And this means to refuse "to sit on information simply because it's not intellectually respectable information" (188). One has to refuse to become like those wealthy vacationers – "people who [like] their reality to follow their thoughts" (189). Thought that follows reality will not simply recoil from the Holocaust or from cannibalism (193).

The first part of Ravelstein is about moral or political virtue – especially its culmination in greatness of soul. The second part is about friendship. The third is about philosophy. Chick's memoir of Abe Ravelstein thus imitates the structure of Aristotle's *Nicomachean Ethics*, which provides three successive versions of the exemplary life: the life of moral virtue, the life devoted to friendship (that good without which no one would choose to live even having all the others), and the god-like autonomy of the contemplative life. Perhaps this imitation is intentional; perhaps it is simply the result of Bellow's deep reflection on the fault lines beneath even the very best of lives that determine the pieces into which they tend to break apart. In Bellow, as in Aristotle, these three pieces do not easily make a coherent whole; the best of lives threatens to be either a comic or a tragic impossibility.

Ravelstein's *megalopsuchia* proves rather comical, for it often borders on megalomania. When his neighbors from the floors above and below come to his door to complain because he is playing Rossini at all hours at top volume on his $10,000 speakers, Abe says rather too smugly that "without music you couldn't swallow what life offered, and that it would do them good to submit and listen" (52). It never seems to occur to him that "these little bourgeois types" might rather choose on their own what they will listen to. It's hard to listen to Rossini and Mozart at the same time. And, of course, neither does it occur to him that one of them might be trying to think through a complicated problem in mathematics or perhaps even political philosophy. Chicago, it seems, isn't big enough for two *megalopsuchoi*, who wonder at nothing and for whom nothing is great.

It is not always easy to distinguish Ravelstein's love of the fine from love of fashion. Part of him holds the idols of the cave in contempt; part of him is an idolater. So, on the one hand he demands that his students break free from conventional family ties, and on the other he proceeds to fashion them into a family – his "set."

> Ravelstein had produced (indoctrinated) three or four generations of students. Moreover, his young men were mad for him. They didn't limit themselves to his doctrines, his interpretations, but imitated his manners and tried to walk and talk as he did. . . . (58–59)

And when he is bedridden just before his death he is comforted when he sees those who have come to visit, "people with whom he was familiar, with whom he had affinities – something like relatives – the nearest thing to a family available" (158). He finds the Bloomsbury intellectuals snobbish and would condemn them as gossips were he himself not so fond of gossip. "When I do it," says Ravelstein referring to his willingness to reveal virtually any confidence, "it's not gossip, it's social history" (65). If Ravelstein's attachments are serious, on the basis of his own standards, they are too conventional; if they are ironic, then they are too self-forgiving. In either case they lack intellectual honesty. Loving life too much to be sufficiently hard on himself, he does not really approach the world with an open mind. He is insufficiently philosophic. The *megalopsuchos* takes pleasure in his own goodness, but, as he wonders at nothing, he has not sufficiently thought through the ground for his own high opinion of himself. He is a creature of the very conventionality that he holds in contempt.

On the other hand, neither is Ravelstein a solitary contemplative. Rosamund tells her husband "He's far more sociable than you, Chick. He enjoys company" (152), and Ravelstein himself says "Nature and solitude are poison" (154). In order to chide Chick for spending summers in New Hampshire, his "quiet green retreat where [he] think[s] and work[s]" (110), Ravelstein quotes Socrates in the *Phaedrus* on how the trees have nothing to teach him (100). Later he remarks on Chick's tendency to "check out the externals": "You can count on nature doing what nature has been doing forever. Do you think you are going to rush in on Nature and grab off an insight?" (177). As a "political philosopher" (231), Ravelstein devotes "himself mainly to the two poles of human life – religion and government" (178); "he [has] little interest in natural life. Human beings absorbed him entirely" (142). This is certainly of a piece with philosophy that has been brought "down from the heavens and into the cities to treat the human things," but only so long as the human things are understood to be the true objects of contemplation. That this is not quite what Ravelstein has in mind becomes clear in his criticism of Chick's attachment to nature: "Can you explain what Nature does for you – a Jewish city type?" (110) "For miles around you're the only Jew" (116). To be a Jew is to be a man of the city, and yet "on our own side of the Atlantic . . . as a Jew you are also an American, but somehow you are also not" (23).

Jerusalem and Athens are not Chick's dish, but in the end he cannot avoid them if he is to give an accurate report of Ravelstein. If

Ravelstein "had to choose between Jerusalem and Athens . . . , he chose Athens" (173). Sight – *theôria* – trumps obedience. Ironically, being a Jew prepares one for Socratic philosophy; one knows as a birthright what it means to belong but somehow also not belong. Ironic detachment is the necessary condition for philosophy. And yet Ravelstein's Jewishness is more than the prolegomenon to philosophy: "In his last days it was the Jews he wanted to talk about, not the Greeks" (173). Similarly, when Chick struggles to begin the memoir he promised to write, Rosamund tells him that he has been avoiding the most important problem – the Jewish question (167). In general and in particular this proves to mean that "it is impossible to get rid of one's origins, it is impossible not to remain a Jew" (179). Accordingly, it is impossible to be simply or purely an observer. Ravelstein is a political philosopher with a certain contempt for the merely natural because mere nature is an illusion. In this regard he and Chick agree: "The gray net of abstraction covering the world in order to simplify and explain it in a way that served our cultural ends has *become* the world in our eyes"; what is needed is "a gift for reading reality – the impulse to put your loving face to it and press your hands against it" (203). Putting one's face to nature, then, means looking at human beings, or perhaps parrots.

Only once in the book does Ravelstein show any interest in nature. Encountering a flock of parrots – tropical birds that have escaped captivity and having adapted to Chicago winters live in nests that remind Chick of tenements, he says "They even have a Jew look to them" (141–42, 169–70, 233). Only in their movement away from nature do beings become interesting to him. Of Ravelstein's "peculiar Jewish face," Chick says "You couldn't imagine an odder container for his odd intellect" (173). If it seems impossible to imagine a non-Jewish Ravelstein, is this not to say that the very thing that initially prepares him for the contemplative life ultimately guarantees its imperfect realization? Ravelstein loves company but not simply for the sake of contemplation. Nikki is his heir.

We are told early on that Ravelstein wrote a "difficult but popular" book, and that "it is no small thing to become rich and famous

by saying exactly what you think" (4). In his way, Ravelstein combines political virtue and intellectual virtue; he is at once great-
souled and contemplative. And yet, the two can exist neither sepa-
rately nor together. The great-souled man is insufficiently attentive
to the artificiality of the content of his love – too quick to dismiss
mud, hair, and dirt – to be really great-souled. The contemplative is
insufficiently attentive to the fact of his own love – too quick to
accept philosophy – to be really contemplative. Furthermore, even
this pseudo-detachment is at odds with the pseudo-grandeur of the
great-souled. On the one hand, Ravelstein knows this; he never
claims to be a philosopher and his love of the *kalon* is deeply ironic. On the other hand, he represents the profound longing to put
together these two halves of our humanity. As in Aristotle's
Nicomachean Ethics, the problematic togetherness of these two is
somehow represented by friendship.

If the conventionality of fame, of oneself as a phenomenon available to the world, is necessarily at odds with the naturalness of genuine thought, of oneself as a thing in itself, perhaps the limited audience of the friend can bridge the gap between the two. The friend is
the other for whom one can be simply what one is – one's self.
Although Chick is a little doubtful, from Ravelstein's point of view
they are friends because "there's nothing I say to you that you don't
immediately understand" (117), and even Chick himself says that
"friendship would not have been possible if we hadn't spontaneously understood each other" (11). After Ravelstein's death Chick
"began to see that it had become [his] habit to tell him what had happened since we last met" (188). Yet, while it was their sense of what
was funny that bound them together (118), "the fact that we laughed
together didn't mean that we were laughing for the same reasons"
(14). Chick sees that "the simplest of human beings is . . . esoteric
and radically mysterious" (22), and the two agree that "when you
destroy a human life you destroy an entire world – the world as it
existed for that person" (156). The sign that these two souls are not
altogether married is marriage. Twice Chick withholds information
from Ravelstein – once about Vela and once about his intention to
marry Rosamund. First Rosamund:

> I wasn't going to have Ravelstein vet Rosamund for me. I couldn't let him arrange my marriage as he did for his students. If he lacked all feeling for you, he didn't give a damn what you did. But if you were one of his friends it was a bad idea, he thought, for you to take things into your own hands. It troubled him greatly to be kept in the dark on any matter by his friends – especially by those he saw daily. (90)

and,

> . . . he had been taken by surprise when he learned that in marrying Rosamund I had not bothered to consult him. I was willing to admit that he might know more about me than I myself knew, but I was not about to put myself in his custody and rely on him to run my life for me. It would also be unjust to Rosamund. (139)

Of Vela, Ravelstein remarks,

> You gave in – you tried to sell me a colored cutout of the woman like the cardboard personalities they used to hang in movie lobbies in the old days. You know, Chick, you sometimes say there's nothing you can't tell me. But you falsified the image of your ex-wife. You'll say that it was done for the sake of marriage but what kind of morality is *that*? (176)

So the two are not perfectly one. And it is Ravelstein's own understanding of marriage that accounts for the incompleteness:

> People are beaten at last with their solitary longings and intolerable isolation. They need *the* right, *the* missing portion to complete themselves, and since they can't realistically hope to find that they must accept a companionable substitute. Recognizing that they can't win, they settle. (120)

More than he admits, Ravelstein's philosophical friendship with Chick, their "marriage of true minds," is of this sort and, therefore, in tension with the other marriages of Chick, who is a "serial marrier."

Out of friendship Chick agrees to write a biography of Ravelstein. The task ought to be easy if they are true friends, for Chick should know Ravelstein inside out. But he can't do it. When he comes close to dying himself, explicitly likens his disease to

Ravelstein's (190, 224), and finally criticizes Ravelstein's under-standing of love (the conviction that "figures in all his judgments" – 140), in coming to self-understanding, Chick can finally give an account of Ravelstein. It is the difference between them that proves to make the difference. Rosamund, who "loved Ravelstein" and "was one of his great admirers" (41), who according to Ravelstein was "earnest, hard-working, had a good mind" but was disabled for philosophy because of a natural female longing for children, mar-riage, and the stability of family life (140) and about whom in the early days of their marriage Chick "discovered that, in having her way, she put [his] interests ahead of her own," knows "far more about [love] than either her teacher [Ravelstein] or her husband" (231). Chick's life is saved by his wife, a woman totally devoted to him, on Thanksgiving – "a family day" (205). Ravelstein, who "hated his own family and never tired of weaning his gifted students from their families" (50), for all his talk of Aristophanic eros, never quite acknowledges its hold over him. "Ravelstein urged his young men to rid themselves of their parents. But in the community that formed around him his role became, bit by bit, that of a father" (27). There is a certain self-ignorance about Ravelstein – he once says to his friend, "That's not my style, Chick, to lay down the law" (154) – that both enables his soul to long for the good in all its complexity and at the same time places him deeply at odds with himself. Friendship, which seems at first to offer the possibility of resolving the tension between the political and philosophical lives, in the end reflects this tension within itself in a dual demand – on the one hand, tyrannically dissolving another into oneself and on the other, self-lessly dissolving oneself into another. In the end Chick wants to say that the latter is the deeper, and that Abe Ravelstein was better for not having lived up to his own self-understanding.

Chick's "personal metaphysics," to which he several times refers, has to do with acknowledging the hold the world has on us despite our attempts to break free. Ravelstein's great virtue was that when you became set in your ways, seeing "nothing original, nothing new," "he turned your face again toward the original. He forced you to reopen what you had closed" (180). But despite, or perhaps because of, this virtue something remains closed in him. What qualifies Chick to write a memoir of Ravelstein is that his specialty is not "scientific speculation" but "ordinary daily particulars" – the phenomena and not the noumena or "things in themselves" (195). Ravelstein and Rosamund both chide him for too often getting lost in the details, but for Chick God is quite literally in the details – "You couldn't study a Caribbean evening sky without thinking of God" (197). What this means is that the phenomena have an unbreakable claim on us. After he has recovered Chick has the following conversation with Rosamund:

> "Why would it always be the *worst* things which appear to you so real? Sometimes I wonder if I'll ever be able to talk you out of being so sadistic to yourself.
>
> "Yes," I agreed. "It has a specific kind of satisfaction, the bad of it guarantees it as real experience. This is what we go through, and it's what existence is like. The brain is a mirror and reflects the world. Of course we see pictures, not the real things, but the pictures are dear to us, we come to love them even though we are aware of how distorting an organ the mirror-brain is." (218–19)

The painful seems more real, and so more valuable; it gives us the impression that only its reality could justify our love of this picture. If we mean by death that "the pictures stop," and if the very act of picturing involves the love of the pictures, then to be alive is to love life. This is what Chick means when he says that despite our atheism, apparently the precondition for philosophy, it is a condition of having the pictures we love that we cannot imagine them stopping. Chick wonders whether anyone believes that the grave is all there is since "no one can give up on the pictures." When we are in our "atheist-materialist" mode, "we just *talk* tough" (122–23). This is the personal metaphysics that Ravelstein repeatedly attempted to wean him from. In the end Chick places Rosamund above Ravelstein because she exemplifies it less grudgingly than their mutual teacher, who for all his talk of *eros*, is in the end out of a will to have it all proves to be insufficiently erotic.

A final word. It is by now obvious that I have yet to mention the name, Allan Bloom. Of course, it is beyond question that Saul

Bellow used Bloom as a model for Ravelstein. But, as I recollect, though a moderately big man, Bloom was nowhere near six and a half feet tall. Bellow seems to have consulted the pieces of the nature of the real Allan Bloom to paint his picture of Abe Ravelstein in whom these pieces are exaggerated to tragic proportions. But even were this portrait meant to represent the admittedly larger than life Allan Bloom, it would be odd to find fault, for Bellow would have done his friend the honor of displaying in him the highest features of our humanity in the complexity of their relations with one another. Even if the pieces of Allan Bloom were at odds, that the pieces should be greatness of soul, the love of wisdom, and friendship is praise of a very high order and proof of why you don't easily give up a creature like Allan Bloom to death.

Part Three

BOOKS AND TEACHING

Chapter 13

THE PHILOSOPHY OF LEO STRAUSS: AN INTRODUCTION[1]

I was asked to speak this evening on the philosophy of Leo Strauss. I do this with a certain reluctance for two reasons. First, although I heard Strauss speak only a few times, my own teachers – Allan Bloom who sold me on the philosophic life, Richard Kennington who taught me what it meant, and Seth Benardete who was for me its full embodiment – were all among his first students (before there were any "Straussians"). On the one hand, then, Strauss is in my blood; everything I think has been influenced by him, although I hasten to add that he ought not be held accountable for the results. On the other hand, because Strauss is a thinker of a very high order, one ought to study him the way one studies other such thinkers – carefully and, as Seth Benardete once said, "surren-der[ing] to authority while fighting all the way."[2] To speak about Strauss under any circumstances would be a challenge. For me, the task recalls my undergraduate education in philosophy in a depart-ment filled with followers of Ludwig Wittgenstein but never offer-ing a course on Wittgenstein, who was too much present in every-thing they did to make that very presence an object of inquiry. Self-

1 Originally given at the State University of New York at New Paltz, spring 2004.
2 "Interpreting Plato's *Charmides*," in *The Argument of the Action*, 243.

knowledge is hard. All this was in my mind when David Blankenship asked whether I would come to New Paltz to speak about Strauss, and all this made me hesitant to accept. You deserve someone who has studied Strauss more thoroughly.

Why then am I here? This brings me to my second reason for reluctance. Strauss is much in the news of late. Tim Robbins, the unforgettable Ebby Calvin "Nuke" Laloosh of *Bull Durham* fame, has recently authored, directed, and produced a play entitled *Embedded* at the Public Theater in New York City. The play traces the Iraq policy of the Bush Administration to a group of neo-conservatives who self-consciously understand themselves to be Straussians; they apparently address the words "Hail Strauss" to an image of him projected on the wall. This is, of course, a strange fate for a Jewish refugee from Hitler's Germany who, although a critic of modernity, was also a life-long defender of liberal democracy against the reigning ideologies of both the right and the left. There is a certain irony in the fact that Strauss, for whom the early modern project of politicizing philosophy was perhaps the greatest threat to politics and to philosophy, should stand accused of politicizing philosophy, and so himself become an "idol of the cave." He deserves better. Yet he is unlikely to receive better, for a defense of Strauss would really require a thorough defense of what he, more than perhaps any thinker since Plato, made the centerpiece of his thought – the philosophic life. And, even for Plato, the philosophic life was so elusive in its nature as to require multiple accounts, each in an extremely indirect form. My second reason for reluctance, then, is my suspicion that what I have agreed to do is really impossible in the time and in the form that I have agreed to do it. Still, here I am, attempting do something impossible for which I am in any case admittedly ill-equipped. This sort of thing is generally called moral obligation.

I. The Crisis of Modernity

Strauss is most obviously a political philosopher. This in a way simplifies the task of introducing his thought, for one of his early works is entitled *What is Political Philosophy?* It seems reasonable then to follow his lead and turn first to his account of the class to which he belongs in order to understand how he fits within it. Political philosophy is about politics. All political action, Strauss points out, aims either at preservation or at change. The one looks to make things better, the other to keep them from becoming worse. Accordingly all political action is guided by some thought of better and worse, and so finally by thought about what is good. Now, these thoughts about what is good are, on the one hand, the most important thoughts that we have and, on the other, the most open to question. They have the character of opinions. Still, that we can question them makes us aware of the possibility of thoughts about the good that would be no longer subject to question and so would have the character not of opinion but of knowledge. Such knowledge is what all political action implicitly invokes – i.e., knowledge of what is simply and without question good as a measure of what makes human life and so the society organized to enhance human life good. Now, *every* society embodies and even articulates some notion of what is good by which it measures itself and others, but society seldom if ever self-consciously recognizes this notion let alone *questions* it. This is what differentiates ideology, the sense that one has the truth, from philosophy, genuinely seeking it, for "the distinctive trait of the philosopher," Strauss says, "is that he 'knows that he knows nothing,' and that his insight into our ignorance concerning the most important things induces him to strive with all his power for knowledge" (*WPP?*, 11). Here he identifies philosophy by the Socratic formula for philosophy – knowledge of ignorance; political philosophy is on the surface at least, a branch of it.

Granting the obvious importance of the knowledge sought by political philosophy – knowledge of the comprehensive human good – Strauss calls to our attention a startling fact: "Today," he says, "political philosophy is in a state of decay and perhaps of putrefaction, if it has not vanished altogether" (*WPP?*, 17). Two hundred and fifty years ago it would have been unthinkable for a major philosopher to say nothing about politics; now this omission is the rule.[3] The fundamental question of political philosophy (the nature of the best form of government, the best *regime*) has been discredited. It is thought naïve – either because unscientific or unhistorical. This pair of charges teaches us something about ourselves, for it brings to light the two powerful standards that govern us in our age, for the most part unwittingly: Science and History.

The rejection of political philosophy as unscientific has its source in positivism, which in turn has as its fundamental principle the distinction between facts and values. According to positivism, the question of the best regime and others like it are questions of value, but only questions of fact are empirically verifiable and thus subject to rational inquiry. Such questions fall within the domain of science; all else is subjective. Questions of beauty, goodness, and justice thus reduce to irrational preferences. This view, while superficially less dominant than it was when Strauss wrote the first version of "What is Political Philosophy?" in 1954, remains very powerful today. We pay lip service to anti-scientific theories – we deconstruct the scientific world view – but we still rush to medical specialists when we are seriously ill. The fact/value distinction regularly shows up in the division in colleges and universities between the hard sciences and the soft humanities and in the sometimes comical efforts of the soft social sciences to appear hard.

There are, however, superficial reasons to be suspicious of this distinction. How could one ever show it to be true? Were it self-evident, it would always have been thought true, but it seems to be of rather recent origin – it is a nineteenth-century "discovery." And, of course, it is not really obvious to us in our ordinary lives, for we act all the time as though we knew certain values to be true. Intellectuals, inclined to challenge this claim, are perhaps the greatest culprits, for they do not doubt for a moment that it is better to be an intellectual than not. Now since whatever empirical evidence there is does not seem obviously on the side of the fact/value distinction, and since, according to positivism and the science it takes as a paradigm for knowledge, all truth depends on empirical evi-

3 Strauss cites as examples Bergson, Whitehead, Husserl, and Heidegger – he would not have considered John Rawls an exception.

dence, we are allowed, even compelled, to ask where the factual datum is that corresponds to the distinction between facts and values. If it does not exist, then the distinction is unscientific – itself a mere value preference – and we need not take it seriously unless we have an irrational inclination to do so. The point is that facts are not natural entities floating free in the world. They are answers to questions. These questions come from us, and we ask some questions and not others because we have an advance notion that their answers will be valuable to us. This sense does not come from science but from a pre-scientific view of the world that science, and especially social science, can never simply leave behind. Strauss frequently used a small but not insignificant example: since the conclusions of social science are about human beings, in order to begin at all social scientists must be able to differentiate human beings from all the other beings that exist, thereby always assuming knowledge for themselves, and for those whom they address, of what a human being is. To the extent, then, that modern social science takes positivism as a paradigm and seeks a value-free knowledge of values, it undermines the very thing it thinks it seeks to understand. Accordingly Strauss can say in another context that social science fiddles while Rome burns, although, he suggests, it may be excused by two facts: "it does not know that it fiddles, and it does not know that Rome burns" (*LAM*, 223).

These difficulties internal to positivism point to what Strauss considers the deeper of the two contemporary ideologies – historicism. That we tend to understand things historically is clear from a quick glance at any college catalogue, where more often than not courses are categorized historically – think not only of "19th Century Philosophy" but also of "Modern Dance." The power of historicism is first that it readily acknowledges that facts exist only within a structure of values and makes the further observation that this structure, or horizon, within which we view our world, and according to which we understand the good and the bad, the beautiful and the ugly, the just and the unjust, and, most importantly, even the true and the false, varies according to the historical epoch in which we live. This view has become so common in our age that we regularly compare our values to, say, the values of the sixties or the eighties. Now, to claim that values are historically relative does not at first seem so novel. The very Odysseus who in his wanderings "saw the towns of many men and knew their mind" (*Odyssey*, I.3), Strauss notes, is the first character known to us in the literature of the West to learn of the distinction between convention and nature – *nomos* and *phusis*. It is interesting that this discovery, necessary for philosophy to come to be at all, is present from the very outset of the Western tradition. Strauss once remarked in a letter that "some day my belief that Homer started it all and that there was a continuous tradition until the end of the 18th century will be vindicated."[4] Yet, as Odysseus – not to mention Herodotus and Heracleitus – does not seem to have been an historicist, *noticing* the discrepancy between *nomos* and *phusis* and hence the variety of ways in which human beings live need not mean embracing historical relativism. One may believe that human moralities are generally, or even necessarily, conventional and still think it possible to penetrate through these conventions to get at the truth about human beings – their nature. In generally identifying the human good with the pleasant, for example, ancient conventionalism preserved the possibility of philosophy as a transconventional inquiry into nature.

Historical relativism, itself, comes in two versions – naïve and radical (*NRH*, 25, 32). Naïve historicism first emerges in opposition to doctrines "regarded as final in all important respects" (*NRH*, 22); it seems a reasonable response to the dangers of dogmatic universalism. Noticing the extremes to which those who think themselves to possess knowledge of universally valid principles are prone – the terror of the French Revolution, for example – we become skeptical of the value of such principles.

> But dogmatism – or "the inclination to identify the goal of our thinking with the point at which we have become tired of thinking" [Strauss is quoting Lessing here] – is so natural to man that it is not likely to become a preserve of the past. (*NRH*, 22)

---

4   Letter to Seth Benardete, November 15, 1957.

Dogmatism thus takes up new quarters in the anti-dogmatic dogma of historical relativism. What was initially the result of a healthy suspicion of political and moral certainty recasts itself as absolute certainty about the impossibility of certainty. The result, rather than furthering thought, lazily, and dogmatically, truncates it. While naïve historicism first presents itself as a simple reflection on experience, in fact it contains within it the germ of the universalism to which it is so opposed. Its celebration of the diversity and uniqueness of historical epochs is merely a variation on the high value placed on the uniqueness of the individual in the Enlightenment philosophy that it believes itself to reject. This goes hand in hand with a suspicion of reason, which, in understanding things, must always grasp them in so far as they belong to a class – a kind. Naïve historicism is, despite itself, a principled doubt of principles.

This problem may be put in another way. Naïve historicism claims to know of the relativity of all value over time. But one is moved to wonder how such knowledge – presumably theoretical and transhistorical – is possible in the world as historicism describes it. Radical historicism distinguishes itself from naïve historicism by facing this problem head on and refusing to acknowledge the transhistorical character of its insight into the historical relativity of all value. That is, truth itself becomes available only from within an historical context, which is to say truth becomes unavailable. Radical historicism calls into question the very possibility of philosophy and hence of political philosophy.

This is our situation. Strauss calls it the crisis of modernity. It shows itself in a variety of ominous ways. The result of our "knowledge" of the relativity of all value is that we are reluctant to assert our own values or to allow others the assertion of theirs. This may at first seem to be good news marking a new era of civilization in which, for example, the bloody religious wars of earlier eras will be forestalled. This new age would be an age of pluralism – of tolerance of a variety of values. But the good news quickly turns bad in a double way. On the one hand, where there is no longer anything worth dying for, it is not clear that there is anything worth living for. It is therefore not clear how seriously to take an age that no longer permits one to become outraged by anything other than becoming outraged. Furthermore, it is not clear how reasonable this moralistic move to tolerance actually is, for tolerance would be, according to historical relativism, a view like all others – no better no worse. We are therefore left with two possibilities – neither particularly attractive. Either we have no reason to embrace one value over another, our wills are sapped of all energy, and we are perilously close to a paralyzing nihilism; or we fatalistically submit to whatever view is currently dominant, so that what is most powerful in the present hijacks the claim to be true as well. In both cases political life is brutalized. For Strauss, then, modernity is in crisis because it is threatened by a self-understanding that by denying legitimacy to the question "What is good?" threatens us from two sides, either eroding or inflating our self-confidence, and with equally fatal results. The two dangers are in a way Weimar and Nuremberg. A sign, perhaps *the* sign, of this crisis is the decay of political philosophy, which is, in turn, a sign of the decay of genuine, that is to say Socratic, philosophy – philosophy rooted in knowledge of ignorance. Strauss was fond of quoting Pascal's remark that "we know too little to be dogmatists and too much to be skeptics." For Leo Strauss the recovery of the possibility of philosophy is a matter of the greatest import, for what is at stake is nothing less than our humanity. It is not, as Heidegger had thought, the problem of being that we have forgotten. It is the problem of natural right. Strauss is a political philosopher for whom an awareness of the *problem* of the good is understood to *be* the good in the light of which all else is measured. While the restoration of an awareness of the problem of the good is of some urgency, it is not difficult to see why this urgency does not lend itself to ideology.

This restoration is especially difficult in the present because, while political life always exists in an atmosphere of taken-for-granted opinions – what Strauss, following Plato, likens to a cave where we mistake shadows for reality – our cave has been unnaturally darkened by the alliance that the Enlightenment sought to forge between philosophy and political life. We understand our practical lives in ways thoroughly saturated with theoretical terms – our problems are "psychological" not "psychic," our woes owing to "history" or to "society." I once witnessed an argument over a parking place in New York City where one livid person, at wit's end, finally screamed at another "you paranoid psychotic"; in another age he might have said "you god-damned bastard." We speak of our lives so abstractly that we inhabit what Strauss calls a "cave beneath the cave" – twice removed from reality. Preliminary excavation is, therefore, required simply to ascend to the cave in order to recover the perspective from which people ordinarily misunderstand themselves, the perspective that is the beginning point for all genuine questioning.[5]

II. Ancients and Moderns

Now, if the crisis of our time is the crisis of modernity, the situation in which we find ourselves cannot be the permanent condition of human beings. Something decisive must have changed, and so the task of recovering the possibility of philosophy involves understanding this change. Accordingly we are in need of both an historical inquiry into the genesis of the crisis of modernity and a philosophical inquiry into the shape of its alternatives. The two prove difficult to separate.

The historical origin of modernity, for Strauss, seems at first to have three signature elements: the decline of religion, the new science, and the new political philosophy.[6] Yet modern natural science is meant from its founding as an alternative to Aristotelian physics and is expressly designed to be neutral to ends or purposes – "that species of cause termed final." But, as science is not equipped to address the goals of the movement of which it is such an instrumental part, the core of modernity is not so much the methodology of its most prominent product as a novel reflection on the nature of the human good – a political philosophy – that gives rise to this methodology. Not Descartes but Machiavelli is the true founder of

---

5   We must make a "special effort to attain to the distinction, which is at the heart
    of philosophy, between those things which are first for us and those things
    which are first by nature." Seth Benardete, Untitled typescript, 1974, 1.
6   See Richard Kennington, "Leo Strauss and Modernity," typescript, 1974, 1.

modernity, and the new science, while enormously important in
terms of its consequences for our daily lives, is not the essence of
the historical change that Strauss seeks to understand. Still, this science – established so that by means of our own reason we might
make ourselves "like masters and owners of nature" and be released
from the burdens of old age and of labor (i.e., from the curse laid on
Adam and Eve when they are expelled from paradise) – points in a
powerful way to what does animate modernity: the ideal of the
autonomous individual. As the new masters of nature, we will perforce replace the old; accordingly modern philosophy is at its origin
at odds with revealed religion. It is animated by an ire at once anti-
theological and anti-teleological. Because it sets as a goal not obedience to, but imitation of, a creator god, it is no longer willing to
look to nature as the source of our knowledge of human ends and
purposes.

Of the elements of modernity both the new science and the
decline of religion are derivative. Accordingly, the true origin of
modernity is the new political philosophy, which, as it appears first
in Machiavelli, Hobbes, and even Descartes, is consciously formulated in opposition to antiquity. The historical inquiry into the origin
of modernity therefore requires a philosophical reconsideration of
what was uniformly rejected by its founders, even if only to understand the reasons for this rejection. Ancients versus moderns is thus
the first of several dyads that must be won through in grappling with
Strauss's thought. At the same time, in opposing the prevailing view
of its age, modernity is founded on a fundamental opposition to the
teachings of Biblical religion and especially of Christianity. To
understand our situation, then, along with the quarrel between
ancients and moderns, we must also think through the quarrel
between Athens and Jerusalem – reason and faith. And, since, to
understand Athens, one must most of all understand Plato (to whom,
according to Alfred North Whitehead, all of Western philosophy is
nothing more than a series of footnotes), and since at the heart of
Plato's thought is the "ancient quarrel between philosophy and poetry," the third dyad at the heart of Strauss's thought is poetry versus
philosophy.

Modern political philosophy sets itself against both Biblical religion and ancient philosophy. Because it claimed victory in the latter contest – i.e., because it claimed to be the true philosophy and so to speak for philosophy *tout court* – the more fundamental tension seems to be Athens versus Jerusalem. Strauss often seems to agree with this ordering, for while in the apparently intramural philosophic quarrel he allies himself with the ancients, it is not so clear where he stands with respect to the alternative reason versus faith. He often seems to argue that the choice cannot be rational.[7] In thus leaving open the question of philosophy's ability to justify the goodness of the philosophic life, Strauss would abandon his criterion for measuring the good society. This reminds us of the beginning "What is Political Philosophy?" where Strauss leaves intact the introduction from his original lecture. Speaking in Jerusalem, he tells his audience that he "shall not forget for a moment what Jerusalem stands for" where the "theme of political philosophy – 'the city of righteousness, the faithful city' – has been taken more seriously than anywhere else on earth." Yet he ends the first part of the same essay with the following remark.

> The biggest event of 1933 would rather seem to have proved, if such proof was necessary, that man cannot abandon the question of the good society, and that he cannot free himself from the responsibility for answering it by deferring to History or to *any other power different from his own reason*. (*WPP?*, 27 – italics mine)

This is consistent with another of Strauss's essays, "Jerusalem and Athens," where after cautioning us lest "by saying we wish to hear first and then to act to decide, we have already decided in favor of Athens against Jerusalem" (*JA*, 5), he proceeds to inquire at length into the philosophical meaning of the first chapter of Genesis, which he says "begins reasonably" (*JA*, 7). Here, Strauss displays in deed, even if questioning in speech (out of a spirit of prudence and genuine deference) a fundamental trust in reason. Now, if, as Strauss

---

7   See "Progress or Return?" in *The Rebirth of Classical Political Rationalism: An Introduction to the Thought of Leo Strauss*, 270.

was fond of remarking, Nietzsche was right that we understand an atheist by understanding what god it is that he does not believe in, is it possible that in seeking to defeat both ancient philosophy and Biblical religion, modern political philosophy ends up simultaneously mirroring both so as to combine them, "blurr[ing] henceforth the essence of philosophy and religion"?[8] That is, is the stark alternative faith versus reason part of the legacy of the modern project to make philosophy practical which therefore places philosophy and religion on the same plane? Is this dyad part of the politicizing of philosophy characteristic of the cave beneath the cave? Should something like this be the case, then Strauss's attempt to recover the natural beginnings of philosophy is an attempt to recover a mode of questioning more fundamental than the "choice" between religion and philosophy as understood by modernity. Ancients versus moderns would be on a deeper plane than Athens versus Jerusalem in the sense that understanding the former adequately would fundamentally change our understanding of the latter. What then does Strauss mean by ancients versus moderns?

The quarrel between ancients and moderns is at its heart an argument about the nature, goodness, and power of reason. And because the question of human virtue is inseparable from the question of reason, it is a quarrel as well about morality. And because the question of morality, as inseparable from the question of justice, is also inseparable from the question of politics, it is a quarrel as well about politics. Hence Machiavelli's "critique of morality . . . is identical with his critique of classical political philosophy" (*WPP?*, 41). For Plato and Aristotle, human beings are by nature rational animals, the perfection of our natures (full human virtue) consists in the perfection of our distinctive feature (our rationality), and genuine happiness consists in a life of virtuous activity, a life in which the parts of our nature are made whole; the best life is the life according to nature. Now, while "the positive principle animating modern political philosophy has undergone a great variety of changes," these variations "have a fundamental principle in common," which "can best be stat-

8 Kennington, 3.

ed negatively: rejection of the classical scheme as unrealistic" (*WPP?*, 40).

Ancient virtue asks too much of reason. Machiavelli urges us to aim lower so as to achieve more. The Greek philosophers understood that a genuinely good life would require living in a well-ordered political society, for otherwise what we are expected to do for the sake of the common good will be at odds with what is genuinely good. We will be divided against ourselves – alienated. However, such a political order depends for its existence on good human beings; accordingly, Plato and Aristotle understand *the* goal of politics to be education to virtue. At the same time, because they are skeptical of the possibility of realizing this order, they understand human beings to be permanently alienated. Therefore, while ancient political and moral philosophy understands human beings in terms of what is highest in them, and so is idealistic, it is pessimistic about the possibility of reaching these heights. Machiavelli rejects both their idealism and their pessimism by seeking to reinterpret virtue in such a way as to be within reach. The goal will be lower, but attainable. In different ways Biblical religion and philosophy insist on interpreting the low in us in terms of the high – the human in terms of its directedness toward the superhuman.[9] Machiavelli "tended to believe that a considerable increase in man's inhumanity was the unintended but not surprising consequence of man's aiming too high" (*WPP?*, 44). This tendency must be thwarted if we are to gain control over our own lives.

Now, in one way, the ancients are not so different from Machiavelli; for both, the ideal is a certain godlike autonomy or freedom. We have seen that they differ with regard to the ultimate attainability of this end; they differ also with regard to the appropriate means to it. For Machiavelli and those who immediately follow him, human beings do have a nature, but this nature, while governing our behavior, is not reason. We are fundamentally passionate – i.e., selfish beings. This is surely a serious disagreement, but it is not at first clear why it need generate the watershed distinction:

9 Kennington, 4.

Ancients vs. Moderns. There were, after all, philosophers in antiquity for whom pleasure was understood to be the highest good. However, the view of Machiavelli and his heirs represents a radical mutation. It is not just hedonism but political hedonism and is meant to provide the theoretical ground for fundamentally transforming the human situation.

> Machiavelli is the first philosopher who attempted to force chance, to control the future by embarking on a campaign, a campaign of propaganda. This propaganda is the opposite pole of what is now called propaganda, high-pressure salesmanship and hold-up of captive audiences. Machiavelli desires to convince, not merely to persuade or bully. He was the first of a long series of modern thinkers who hoped to bring about the establishment of new modes and orders by means of enlightenment. The enlightenment – *lucus a non lucendo* – begins with Machiavelli. (*WPP?*, 46)

For Machiavelli, education to moral virtue is at best ineffectual and at worst dangerously misleading. The way to autonomy is not to practice virtue by living "according to nature" but rather to use one's ingenuity to contest nature – to master fortune. The means to this end is a new science of politics that by studying the selfish ways in which we actually behave, and by convincing us that there is really no option but to behave as we do, will pave the way for replacing moral virtue as the ground of good politics with tough institutions, new modes and orders, that by acknowledging the power of our passions will in the end maximize their satisfaction and make us happy. If we, Machiavelli's children, do not immediately recognize our own ways in his harsh advice to princes – for example, that a man will sooner forgive the killing of his father than the theft of his patrimony – perhaps we may discover something not altogether different in Madison's remarks in *Federalist 10* about the benefits to political stability of faction or in the celebrated separation of powers. This project, however, requires that men be enlightened about the truth of their natures, that they no longer be seduced by the seeming nobility of moral virtue and of religion. What is required is therefore an unprecedented alliance between politics and philosophy in which philosophy dedicates itself to the noble redefined as the relief of man's estate and to the truth redefined as the effectual truth, both of which are understood to be within reach.

Machiavelli's great experiment was to free men from the constraints of morality so as to reinterpret the political sphere in terms of a symbiotic selfishness; those who see clearly, and whose satisfaction comes from the assertion of the will in the founding of a new order, establish stable conditions within which the rest are content to live. Machiavelli thus sought a fully political solution to the problem of human alienation. In doing so, however, seeing clearly comes to be defined in altogether political terms. But "precisely because it solved the human problem in terms of the political, the modern solution has the arbitrariness which always belongs to the polis."[10] The new philosophy is expert at predicting the movements of the shadows on the cave wall because it reveals the fact, previously hidden from us, that we have projected them there ourselves. We can know them with some certainty because we made them. But such knowledge makes no pretense of releasing us from the cave. Instead it seeks to wean us from our extra-political longings for wholeness and for the eternal; ceasing to be incomplete requires "defining ourselves down" so that we no longer ache to be more than we are.

From Machiavelli the path leads on the one hand to Descartes and the modern scientific project. Here Strauss identified what he called "the hidden kinship between Machiavelli's political science and the new natural science" (*WPP?*, 47) but left it for others to fill in the details – for example, the way in which mathematical physics itself involves a similarly symbiotic project and the extent to which that project involves a willful imposition of a mathematical order on a sometimes recalcitrant nature. Still, however powerful the scientific strand of modernity, Strauss understands it to be secondary and in the service of the political strand, and so he turns to the further development of modern political philosophy in its first wave, especially in Hobbes and Locke, and then to its second wave, its great transformation originating in Rousseau, and finally to its third wave, the ushering in of the crisis of our time by Nietzsche. By character-

10 Kennington, 4.

izing the genesis of modernity in this way, Strauss tacitly likens its progress to the three waves of Plato's *Republic* (Book 5), i.e., to the radical transformations of political life necessary for the perfect city to come to be. The last and largest of the three is for Socrates so apparently absurd that he risks ridicule even in uttering it – i.e., that there will "not be a cessation of evils . . . for cities nor for the human race" until "political power and philosophy happen to be the same" (473d). What the ancients almost certainly understand to be an impossible coincidence becomes for modernity a realizable project. But the political comes to be philosophical and philosophy comes to be political in a decayed form, for ideology masks the natures of both. Thus "the enlightenment proves to be a darkening."[11]

Hobbes modifies Machiavelli's scheme in the democratic direction already tacitly implied by elevating the passions above reason. Once we take our bearings not by how men ought to be – by some nature that defines us but to which we never altogether live up – but by how they are, it becomes difficult to justify distinctions of virtue among men at all. The true founders of political society are "not heroes, if fratricidal and incestuous heroes, but naked, shivering poor devils" (*WPP?*, 48). Nature remains a standard for Hobbes, but it guides us in a negative way, by a fear of violent death so powerful that the human psyche is best understood as in constant flight from it. In Machiavelli the origin of political life is the longing for glory; in Hobbes this pride is exposed as the remnant of the ancient notion of aristocratic virtue. Hobbes replaces it with fear, a passion equally distributed among men, and as a consequence elevates the importance of power as the object of human longing.[12] Power, more truly morally neutral than glory, is the means by which men seek to realize a right to survival that is rooted in a natural passion over which they have no control. The fact of death insults us with our lack of autonomy – we do not, by nature, have power over our own lives. In seeking to gain this power we move out of a hateful state of nature

11 Richard Kennington, "Final Causality and Modern Natural Right" (unpublished typescript), 28.
12 "I put for a general inclination of all mankind a perpetual and restless desire of power after power that ceaseth only in death." See Hobbes, Thomas, *Leviathan*, Part I, Chapter 11.

into a beneficent but artificial political society. In Hobbes and, after him in Locke, "who took over the scheme of Hobbes and changed it in only one point. He realized that what man primarily needs for his preservation is less a gun than food, or more generally, property" (*WPP?*, 49), human beings can be said to demonstrate an extraordinary adaptability. We invent institutions in response to our only negatively fixed natures, but the very success of these institutions suggests it is possible to alter our natures. We are unusually malleable creatures. This first wave generates what Strauss thought to be perhaps the jewel in modernity's crown, for it laid the foundation for liberal democracy – with its stable institutions. At the same time, however, by placing so great an emphasis on human malleability, it prepared the way for the second wave of modernity inaugurated by Rousseau and for its ultimate rejection of the very notion of human nature.[13]

The modern liberal democracies that are the legacy of Hobbes and Locke, based as they are in a negative understanding of our natures, found political society not on virtue or duty but on natural rights. Their goal, therefore, cannot be happiness; it can only be the pursuit of happiness. The only public determination of the good is that certain conditions are necessary for the pursuit of my own good as I understand it. Modern liberal society therefore establishes the sanctity of the private sphere, and luckily so, for the private sphere preserves a place for those virtues that prove necessary for its preservation. Enlightened self-interest brings so much light to the cave that it makes one wonder whether the cave is worth risking one's life for. Liberal society needs what it cannot help but undermine.[14] Because its founding principles entail skepticism of all universal moral claims, modern liberal society is necessarily at odds with all particular religions. It makes an equal place for all only by denying the deepest claims of each. Over time this contradiction at its core tends to erode virtue (now altogether private) and replace it with a pragmatic hedonistic calculus.

13 Kennington, 5.
14 Kennington, 6.

Rousseau foresaw this tension between virtue and political hedonism and made it the beginning point for his reflection on the inadequacy of the modern rebellion against the ancients. The mixture of reason and passion that constitutes us leads inevitably to our being divided against ourselves – alienated – for our desires are not fixed by nature but are comparative and social. Hobbes and Locke pay too much attention to the pain that we risk from being struck and not enough to the pain that we suffer from the humiliation of being struck. We are passionate creatures, but our passions are molded by reason, and once they become comparative they become in principle infinite and unsatisfiable. Life understood in this way is what Strauss calls a "joyless quest for joy" (*NRH*, 251). Rousseau at first seems intent on restoring something of the ancient notion of virtue, but in fact radicalizes the modern rebellion. Once human wholeness comes to be understood altogether negatively as not being divided against oneself, a rational attack on reason seems reasonable. Whereas Plato measured Athens against Socrates and found it wanting, Rousseau measures reason against civil society and finds reason wanting. If human wholeness in a mythical state of nature is in opposition to reason, then the political solution is a rigid conformism approximating as closely as possible our thoughtless and so "free" mythical condition. The cost of our happiness is therefore the suppression of one side of our nature. Yet, if nature can be suppressed in this way, is it as natural as we had thought? According to Rousseau's account of human nature we are ultimately neither rational nor animal. He must even coin a word for this nature – perfectibility. Human beings are by nature infinitely malleable. Because we take our deepest satisfaction in the act of adapting – it is a manifestation of our freedom—there will always be certain arbitrariness to the ways in which we adapt. This shows up politically in the altogether formal character of Rousseau's fundamental political principle – the general will is curiously neutral to the specific character of the ends that it wills.

The infinite malleability at the core of human nature opens up a possibility that Rousseau had not pursued. The obstacle to human wholeness is the combination of our notion of perfection with what really satisfies us as finite, imperfect beings. But if our natures are essentially malleable, perhaps we can understand their change to be a progress toward the reconciliation of perfection and satisfaction. The second wave of modernity – Rousseau, Kant, Hegel, Marx – while looking back to the ancients for an ideal of wholeness, remains firmly rooted in the realism of modernity for its understanding of satisfaction. If human nature is altogether malleable, perhaps in the changes it undergoes it gradually works through its own alienation transforming itself into something altogether different. For Hegel, the tension between doing and thinking, praxis and theory – or, one might add, politics and philosophy is finally reconciled at the conclusion of a rational process of change – history – when the real and the rational finally coincide. For Marx, history is the process in which we are transformed from partial beings who identify ourselves with only a part of ourselves to whole beings – individuals in the true sense who live in a world that allows us to identify ourselves with all of ourselves. In both cases, we human beings become whole when we live in the just political order. This order, however, "was thought to be established in a manner which contradicts the right order itself" – a way more Machiavellian than Platonic (*WPP?*, 54).

The Rousseauan insight into the malleability of human nature gave way to the understanding of this nature as historical – which is to say, not as natural at all. The first wave of modernity sees nature as a negative standard from which we flee. The second wave, noticing how we transform ourselves in this flight, suggests the possibility that a fixed standard exists by which to measure ourselves at the end of an historical journey. Looking back gives way to looking forward, but in the end this temporalizing of the human, this renunciation of the eternal, can neither be sustained by our ordinary experiences of the world – history does not end – nor, since in its own way it makes an appeal to the atemporal and thus detemporalizes time, can it defend itself or, for that matter, be defended theoretically. In his critique of the historical teachings of his own time, Nietzsche ushers in the third wave of modernity – the wave in which Strauss insists we still live, and which he calls the crisis of our time. The historical process is not rational. Rather "all human life and all human thought ultimately rests on horizon-forming creations which are not susceptible of rational legitimation" and which are the creations of "great individuals" (*WPP?*, 54). Not reason, but the will is the origin of all human creation, and it is a will that confronts a nature that is in no way lawful. The fundamental human experience is one "of suffering, of emptiness, of an abyss" (*WPP?*, 54).

Strauss concludes his history of modernity in "What is Political Philosophy?" with the following:

> Modern thought reaches its culmination, its highest self-consciousness, in the most radical historicism, i.e., in explicitly condemning to oblivion the notion of eternity. For oblivion of eternity, or, in other words, estrangement from man's deepest desire and therewith from the primary issues, is the price which modern man had to pay, from the very beginning, for attempting to be absolutely sovereign, to become the master and owner of nature, to conquer chance. (*WPP?*, 55).

III. Esotericism

Some of you may have noticed that I have talked only very briefly about one of the three dyads in Strauss's thought, Jerusalem and Athens, have gone on at much greater length about another, Ancients and Moderns (but have not really said much about the ancient part of this pair), and have yet to say anything at all about the dyad poetry and philosophy, which I began by saying was the most fundamental of the three. Let me begin to remedy this omission by way of some remarks on what is ordinarily taken to be most controversial about Strauss's thought, his teaching on esoteric and exoteric writing.

In *Persecution and the Art of Writing* (1952), Strauss argues a thesis at that time quite shocking – that in the non-liberal societies of the past, authors were at great pains to write in such a way as to simultaneously conceal their most radical thoughts from religious or political authorities and reveal them to those few who might be able to learn from them. To our democratic age this distinction between the few who understand and the many who do not is particularly troubling. This is no doubt at the root of the present attack on Strauss. One might wonder, however, why we are so shocked at the thought that where something as difficult as the world is to be understood, some will inevitably understand better than others.

According to Strauss, the open, exoteric, or popular teaching was meant to be edifying; the esoteric teaching presented only between the lines was philosophic. If true, of course, this means that received opinions about the meaning of the texts of our tradition are more than likely wrong – and this not *despite* but *because* they are traditional. Strauss suggests that the task of grasping these texts is difficult. We must first never condescend to their authors but rather assume that they knew what they were doing and seek to understand them as they understood themselves. Now, this violates one of the most powerful opinions of our age – our historical sense, which tells us that we must read Machiavelli as a creature of his time. Of course, on the one hand, we got our sense of the age of Machiavelli by reading people like Machiavelli, and, on the other, if we consult our own experience, in our own time we are rather inclined to raise high those authors who are seen to question dominant views and so be at odds with their time. So, the first rule of reading is that one must be deferential. However, authors are never perfect – one can't simply give them a free pass – and so one must question their every move. This is not so much at odds with the rule of deference as it first seems since the best authors write in such a way that only by questioning their every move will we see what they are really doing. The devices of esoteric writing are numerous – but they might in general be called poetic. This is especially true of ancient esotericism, for, as Strauss says, the "typical premodern philosopher . . . is hard to distinguish from the premodern poet" (PAW, 35). One example from a modern author cited by Strauss as practicing esotericism must suffice here. In the fifth paragraph of the first part of the *Discourse on Method*, Descartes tells us to consider his writing a "history or a fable." Two paragraphs later the terms are repeated and we are told that the beauty of fables awakens the mind and, when read with discretion, the memorable actions of histories elevate it and aid in forming our judgment. One paragraph later the terms are repeated again, and we are told that fables make many events seem possible that are not so at all and that even the most faithful histories if they don't change or increase the value of things to make them more worthy of being read at least omit in them all the circumstances that are most base and least illustrious. The rule of deference requires that we take all three of these passages with the same seriousness – we are not allowed to assume that Descartes has become sloppy or lazy. But then we must see that in putting the passages together we are forced to a conclusion that is quite at odds with what we have been led to expect. Descartes openly tells us to read his philosophy poetically. The thinker known as the founder of rationalism and for whom truth is identified with clarity and distinctness then warns us that this means that we need to read his work with considerable discretion and that he will not simply tell us the truth. There may be a tension between philosophy and poetry, but it is not a straightforward opposition. Cartesian philosophy needs poetry. Descartes goes on to indicate (*Discourse,* Part 5) that he is aware of the fate of Galileo at the hands of the Inquisition and that he has tried to avoid Galileo's mistakes (perhaps not the defense of Copernicus so much as being foolish enough to be caught in that defense). The first motive (one might say the exoteric motive) Strauss gives for esotericism is thus fear of persecution. By beginning with persecution Strauss highlights in a very crude way that in illiberal (i.e., non-enlightened) societies at least, where there is a tension between the political world, the cave where opinion rules, and the truth, or at least the attempt to say what is true, there will be a strong motive for esoteric writing. He thus presents as an historical observation a non-historical truth that we who live in a more liberal and pluralistic age would otherwise be uninclined to acknowledge. But if we follow his train of thought carefully we are led to see that "the literary question properly understood is the question of the relation between society and philosophy" (*CAM*, 52). The contemporary incredulity about esoteric writing, which Strauss shows to have become the prevailing view only in the nineteenth century, therefore betrays a certain pronounced optimism about the possibilities of political life perfectly in keeping with the modern enlightenment project. But to the extent that politics as such is always cave-like or illiberal, this crude motive for esotericism, i.e., self-protection, will always exist. Strauss never forgets the fate of Socrates at the hands of the most enlightened civilization of his time.

While Strauss certainly wishes to call our attention to persecution, it is not the sole motive for esotericism, for, as Strauss tells us in the central paragraph of an essay in which he suggests that the central passage of an esoteric writing might be the best place to conceal a revealing statement of the controversial core of its argument, there may be "truths which should not or cannot be pronounced" (*PAW*, 28). They *should not* be pronounced because they will cause harm not only to the writer but perhaps to others less thoughtful for whom the truth that is not understood is really a harmful falsity that they are better off not hearing. So esotericism is practiced not only for the protection of the author but also for the society in which he lives, which, as a society, requires for its existence the general acceptance of certain unconfirmed opinions. Laws against murder cannot be suspended until all of a nation's citizens have adequately answered the theoretical question, What is justice? But more important still, there are truths that *cannot* be pronounced. This is not a prudential or moral issue but a metaphysical issue. Esotericism so understood is at the core of Strauss's understanding of the distinctness of the ancients, of the centrality of political philosophy for them, and of the importance of the ancient quarrel between philosophy and poetry. Seth Benardete puts it as follows:

> There are two kinds of esotericism, ancient and modern. Swift represents one by the bee, which out of the sweet produces the sweet, and the other by the spider, which out of the foulest things produces the most beautiful web. The first kind is metaphysical esotericism, the second political. The first kind necessarily includes the second, the second necessarily denies the first. The first says that it is in the nature of things that things are hidden; the second says that it is in the nature of the city as now constituted that this is so. The second proposes enlightenment, the lightening up of things until nothing and no one are in the dark; the first sets out to disclose things in their hiddenness and show the reality of what appears. Strauss puts this as follows: "The problem inherent in the surface of things and only in the surface of things is the heart of things."[15]

15 "Strauss on Plato," in *The Argument of the Action*, 409.

In approaching the philosophy of Leo Strauss the problem inherent in the surface of things is the problem of esotericism. For both ancient and modern philosophy, the problem of writing is an image of the problem of politics, which is in its turn an image of the problem of being. Ancient philosophy differs from modern insofar as its esotericism is meant as an accommodation to the permanent nature of things. "Being loves to hide"; it reveals itself only indirectly, and therefore its articulation must imitate this indirectness. Philosophy will have an irreducibly poetic element. Modern philosophy, more optimistic, believes that the need for esotericism is "accidental, an outcome of the faulty construction of the body politic, and that the kingdom of general darkness could be replaced by the republic of universal light" (*PAW*, 33). This republic is its project; Strauss never ceased to be moved by its generosity and its audacity. At the same time, he was troubled by the fact that in aiming so high on behalf of humanity modernity was compelled to undermine what most makes humanity worthy of being held high – openness to the permanent nature of things that is the deepest theme of ancient philosophy. It is perhaps best to let Strauss himself describe this openness.

> Philosophy strives for knowledge of the whole. The whole is the totality of the parts. The whole eludes us but we know the parts: we possess partial knowledge of the parts. The knowledge we possess is characterized by a fundamental dualism which has never been overcome. At one pole we find knowledge of homogeneity: above all in arithmetic, but also in the other branches of mathematics, and derivatively in all productive arts or crafts. At the opposite pole we find knowledge of heterogeneity, and in particular of heterogeneous ends; the highest form of this kind of knowledge is the art of the statesman and of the educator. The latter kind of knowledge is superior to the former for this reason. As knowledge of the ends of human life, it is therefore knowledge of a whole. Knowledge of the ends of man implies knowledge of the human soul; and the human soul is the only part of the whole which is open to the whole and therefore more akin to the whole than anything else is. But this knowledge – the political art in the highest sense – is not knowledge of *the* whole. It seems that knowledge of the whole would have to combine somehow political knowledge in the highest sense with the

knowledge of homogeneity. And this combination is not at our disposal. Men are therefore constantly tempted to force the issue by imposing unity on the phenomena, by absolutizing either knowledge of homogeneity or knowledge of ends. Men are constantly attracted and deluded by two opposite charms: the charm of competence which is engendered by mathematics and everything akin to mathematics, and the charm of humble awe, which is engendered by meditation on the human soul and its experiences. Philosophy is characterized by the gentle, if firm, refusal to succumb to either charm. It is the highest form of the mating of courage and moderation. In spite of its highness or nobility, it could appear as Sisyphean or ugly, when one contrasts its achievement with its goal. Yet it is necessarily accompanied, sustained and elevated by *eros*. It is graced by nature's grace.(*WPP?*, 39–40)

The question of humanity is in the end the same as the question of philosophy – the highest possibility for human beings. Philosophy reveals itself most powerfully in its perennial and, in the end, beneficial tension with politics. Philosophy and politics, the deepest of the dyads one encounters in Strauss, is why Seth Benardete once glossed his thought by saying that for Leo Strauss "political philosophy is the eccentric core of philosophy."

Chapter 14

ON OPENING *THE CLOSING OF THE AMERICAN MIND*[1]

When I went off to Cornell University as a seventeen-year-old in 1965, I had two equally powerful ambitions. I wanted to be a nuclear physicist (mine was the Sputnik generation), and I longed to hold high political office. I discovered Allan Bloom in a large lecture class during my sophomore year and began to learn from him something of the meaning of these two longings. Bloom was unusual in the way he mixed together a rigorous study of the texts of the tradition of Western political philosophy with everyday experience – not in the sense of confirming one's experience but in the sense of deepening immeasurably what it meant. We all knew, for example, that we behaved differently to our parents than to others. What we did not know was that this ordinary experience was somehow a sign of a fundamental political predicament – that all political life requires that certain things be unquestioned, a "taking for granted" necessarily at odds with true openness, thinking, or philosophy. My two adolescent ambitions were really one – a longing for distinction which, in turn, was connected to a growing awareness of death. Bloom's gift to me was to help me begin to understand my own

1 Originally presented at Sarah Lawrence College in the fall of 1988 at a colloquium on *The Closing of the American Mind* organized by The Friends of the Library.

passions by way of such things as Plato's analysis of spiritedness and Rousseau's of self-love, which then guided me to matters more important than my own passions. He thereby introduced me to philosophy.

I mention this at such great length because it is, I think, what *The Closing of the American Mind* is about. Rousseau is one of the models for Bloom. The *Emile* seems an account of the necessarily non-bookish character of education. Raising the natural man, the man without prejudices, requires not book-learning but experience. Rousseau therefore teaches everything from geometry to sex by manipulating the experience of his imaginary Emile. Of course all of this is presented to us in a book. Rousseau may not teach Emile to read until he is a teenager, but the true education – *our* education about the importance of experience – comes from a book. Bloom has reflected on Rousseau's example but has seen that our democratic age faces a somewhat different problem. He therefore praises book-learning, but proceeds by way of a rather anecdotal account of his own experience as a teacher. This is surely the most striking feature of *The Closing of the American Mind* – the combination of Mick Jagger and Plato's cave. Following *Emile* and his other great model, Plato's *Republic*, Bloom means to give an account of education as the difficult combination of experience and books. Saul Bellow saw this and imitated Bloom in his foreword to the book.

> Academics, even those describing themselves as existentialists, very seldom offer themselves publicly and frankly as individuals, as persons. So Professor Bloom is a front-line fighter in the mental wars of our times, and as such, singularly congenial to me. (If he can be personal, I see no reason why I should remain the anonymous commentator.) (12)[2]

But why should this combination of books and experience be so difficult? Experience is usually pre-formed by the views prevailing in a given place and time by what the German's call the *Zeitgeist* and the Greeks *doxa*. Genuine education therefore requires becoming aware that one's opinions are only opinions so as to be able to dis-

2 Page numbers follow in parentheses after citations from *The Closing of the American Mind*.

count their distorting influence. This is what Bloom has in mind when he turns to the dominant opinion of our time. Our self-proclaimed virtue – that we are not opinionated but open – is the sign of the closing of the American mind. Openness is for us not a result of inquiry but an assumption we bring to the world – a moral postulate. The result, a passionate belief in the relativity of all passionate beliefs, closes off serious questioning because we "know" in advance that answers are unavailable. Openness is for us a badge we wear not something we seek for. At first glance, then, it looks as though Bloom is simply opposed to relativism; he is an "absolutist." But by pointing to openness as our single virtue – what we bow down before and pride ourselves on – Bloom means to show that education in our time must begin with it.

> For there is no education that does not respond to felt need; anything else acquired is trifling display. (19)

If openness has this character for us, then of course only by examining it in connection with everyday experience could our education be anything else but "trifling display." *The Closing of the American Mind* is a "meditation on the state of our souls" (19) by way of a meditation of the state in which our souls live – America.

Bloom is therefore engaged in exposing our most cherished opinion for what it is, and of course that is annoying. He does so with a certain panache, and that is even more annoying. He begins with students. His is not a very flattering description, but it would be unfair to call it an attack, unless perhaps on teachers and parents. Bloom's account ranges from books to rock music to sex, race, divorce, love, and finally *eros*. He has been called anti-black, anti-woman, anti-democratic, and generally anti-good. It is said that he appeals to a vague general feeling that "things have gone too far" (of course it may be true that things have gone too far). But all of this misses the point as much as the charge of impiety missed the point in the trial and execution of Socrates. Bloom acknowledges, for example, that feminism is a perfectly predictable demand for equality in the polity that celebrates equality. In addition, economic changes and advances in medicine and in technology generally have made the traditional role of women in the family problematic.

> At forty-five [women] were finding themselves with nothing
> to do and forty more years to do it in. . . . In all of these ways
> the feminist case is very strong indeed. (128)

However, feminism is not strong in all ways because it proceeds as though its demand for justice will have no adverse consequences whatsoever. That children will be raised adequately once no parent is exclusively concerned with raising them, that is, once women become as little concerned with childrearing as men have been, is once again a moral postulate – it would be unjust for it not to be true; so it must be true. What Bloom really objects to is the rather naïve view that it automatically follows that righting specific injustices will generate a progressively more moral order. He sees that each step has its adverse effects, effects that do not disappear simply because we refuse to acknowledge them. The problem is that no problem is seen, and in the morally "open" climate of our time no problem is permitted to be seen. This is connected to the "flatness" Bloom sees in the souls of contemporary students. The problem is not that they do not have "values"; it is rather that they do not know what it means not to have them, and therefore do not even long for them. Their souls are insufficiently erotic.

As Bloom means to understand students and not blame them, he provides a long account of the growth of relativism within the tradition of Western philosophy and its peculiar consequences for America. He provides an archeology of certain terms like "charisma," "value," "creativity," "culture," etc. – terms that form the way we think but the use of which has unforeseen consequences. This leads to an "idiosyncratic history" of the university in terms of the perennial tension between politics, or action, and philosophy, or thought. Bloom concludes that the characteristically modern attempt to unite theory and practice ends by threatening to destroy genuine openness. All of this is brought back to his own experience of the anti-philosophic character of the universities since the 1960s – the great celebration of openness that made it unthinkable to say certain things. As the university strove to become more practical and relevant, the same necessity always present in political life came to rule in the universities – that certain things go unquestioned.

Now what does all of this point to? At every stage of his analysis Bloom is at work either bringing old books to bear on contemporary issues or bringing contemporary issues to bear on old books. He could not really mean that our minds are closed, or he would not have bothered to write *The Closing of the American Mind*. His book is therefore meant to be not only a call to education but an example of it. But what sort of example? Bloom's only suggestion for "educational reform," made with considerable qualification as to its efficacy, is a "great books" education. Human beings are always unifying their experience – thinking it together. Even "pluralism" – our openness – is such an attempt at a comprehensive understanding of experience. Almost always, we conform to the most powerful unifying view of our time. Therefore, while this desire for a unified view is at the heart of education, it is also the greatest obstacle to education. The great books provide alternative comprehensive views of experience. For Bloom, the university is where the battle between competing views should be acted out, not where a complacent and dogmatic pluralism should reign. His claim is that the great books facilitate a genuine openness because they represent the results of this passion for a unified view in the greatest thinkers.

What all of this means for colleges and universities is not just that they should teach great books (although they should), but also that the detachment of the book, its apparent alienness from the current and relevant, should be the model for the university itself – not internships, but the ivory tower. In America this is of particular importance, for the taste and thought of the majority wields enormous power in a democracy. In the midst of the celebration of creativity the danger is a slavish conformism – a flatness of soul. Democracy therefore benefits immeasurably from the presence within it of an admittedly elitist institution. The longing for the high and the noble tends to be suppressed by the egalitarian democratic ethos even though the health of democracy requires people who are moved by such longings. Bloom's book therefore suggests a proportion. Books are to experience as the university is to society at large, as Bloom's book in particular is to the contemporary university. In all cases what is required for genuine education is a gadfly –

an alien element within the tradition necessary for the health of the tradition.

The Closing of the American Mind has been attacked from the left as a reactionary call for "traditional values." It has been attacked from the right as insufficiently impressed by the virtues of the American political order. No doubt the book is intended to have political consequences, but in articulating the meaning of "our virtue" Allan Bloom has something more philosophic in mind. In his way he has imitated what Plato's Socrates attempted when detained for an evening in the Piraeus to discuss the question of justice.

Chapter 15

RICHARD KENNINGTON:
THE TRUE AND THE GOOD[1]

According to a first-hand account of Richard Kennington's defense of his doctoral dissertation, which as many of you know did not occur until relatively late in his career, the four members of the committee were each set to ask a question. Hans Jonas, as director, began. Kennington responded by saying "Well, you see, this question has three large parts and each part has three subsections. Let me go through it." He then talked for some forty-five minutes describing the structure of the first question in elaborate detail. This ability to lay out the structure of problems with extraordinary clarity and depth (whether in a prepared lecture or off the cuff in private conversation) was typical of him. One of its minor manifestations was the way he used to map out in advance the structure of the section of text he was about to work through in a seminar. Professors Velkley and McCarthy were both his students.[2] Velkley begins by telling us that for Kennington the crisis of modernity is characterized

1 These comments were originally written for a roundtable on the work of Richard Kennington sponsored by the Claremont Institute at the 2001 American Political Science Association Meeting. At his death in 1999 Kennington was an emeritus professor in the School of Philosophy at Catholic University of America.
2 Both are professors of philosophy in the School of Philosophy at Catholic University of America.

by the loss of the question "Who is the philosopher?" and that this transformation of philosophy has, in turn, two parts: the modern determination of philosophy's end and the modern mode of theoretical analysis – respectively the way up and the way down. McCarthy points to the centrality of the relation between the good and the true in Kennington's understanding of modernity. He then divides this issue into three: esotericism, method, and mastery of nature. They are good students, for like Kennington each understands that thinking involves putting together things that are initially apart and may first appear disparate although in the end they belong together. Let me briefly attempt my own version of this with a view to trying to put together the apparently different questions Velkley and McCarthy raise. What is the connection between the relation of the true to the good, on the one hand, and the question "Who is the philosopher?" on the other?

For Velkley "Who is the philosopher?" is a Socratic question; for McCarthy it is the ancients and medievals who understand the deeper unity of the true and the good. They agree, rightly I believe, that for Kennington Greek philosophy remains the standard against which modern philosophy is to be measured – the ancients are superior to the moderns. They also agree, again rightly, that Kennington never lost sight of the fact that the greatest thinkers of the early modern period were genuine philosophers. Kennington forces us to consider a puzzle; one might formulate it as follows. First, there is a mountain of evidence to demonstrate that Kennington was, to put it in a way that is absurdly minimal, more than competent to write about ancient philosophy.[3] Second, while Kennington was certainly aware of the various crises born of the revolution in philosophy in modernity, his understanding of the heart of this revolution was the unnatural alliance it effected between philosophy and everyday life. And if, as he once said, "the enlightenment proves to be a darkening"[4], there is certainly no reason to believe that this dark cloud can be lifted by further enlightenment. Accordingly, while not unaware

3 See, for example "Two Philosophical Letters," *Review of Metaphysics*, Vol. 53, No. 3, 531–39.

4 "Final Causality and Modern Natural Right," 28.

that some salutary good might arise from his work, Kennington was not one of those who turned to modern philosophy with a view to doing great popular good by exposing its untruth. He took quite seriously the ancient view that philosophy was not the right instrument for transforming political life. But, if the reasons for his preoccupation with modern thought were not primarily moral, and if he readily admitted that it was in the decisive sense inferior to ancient thought, why did Richard Kennington devote so much of his life to the study of modern philosophy? What exactly was its interest for him?

I wondered at first about Velkley's claim that the heart of crisis of European civilization was for Kennington the loss of the Socratic question, Who is the philosopher? and that the problem inherent in the surface of things "refers fundamentally to the natural tension between philosophy and practical life." When Strauss spoke of the problem inherent in the surface of things, one might have thought that he meant that the proper way to understand the being of things is to understand why they must appear as they do – what necessity prevents them from simply appearing as they are. Velkley, however, sees past the surface, for the philosopher must seem strange in his certainty of the provisionality of what everyone else understands as final. If the capacity to see that the surface is only a surface is the distinguishing mark of philosophy, and the necessity to take the surface seriously – as the truth – is what distinguishes practical life, then the modern project, in seeking to make philosophy respectable rather than odd or dangerous, can only succeed by making philosophy seem superficial.[5] As Velkley puts it, "In aiming at universalizable benefits, philosophy as 'Enlightenment' must remove from the center of philosophy the sustained openness to the wondrous which cannot be universalized."

I was at first also perplexed by Velkley's subsequent division of the question of the philosopher in modernity into a consideration of

---

5 Descartes tells us that wonder is useful because it "disposes us to the acquisition of the sciences," but "we ought nevertheless try afterwards to deliver ourselves from it as much as is possible" lest we become too easily astonished at what merits little or no consideration (*Passions of the Soul,* II.76).

the end and mode of analysis of philosophy, for Velkley moves very quickly from a "who" question to a "what" question – from the identity of the philosopher to the nature of philosophy. This is connected to the theme of McCarthy's paper. One might say of the true that to be true means to be true for all or universally but that the good always shows itself as the good for, and this means ultimately what is good for a particular soul. If, as Velkley suggests, the question of the philosopher divides into the question of philosophy's end, its *telos*, and its mode of analysis, its *logos*, it seems fair to say that the whole question, Who is the philosopher? is identical to the question of teleology in its connection to philosophy. Teleology is, of course, at once a claim about goodness and a claim about truth. Kennington's interest in modern philosophy might be said to turn on the question of teleology. What is peculiar to modern philosophy is that it transforms a question aimed at identifying a particular kind of soul into two questions that it knows to be fundamental but is hard-pressed to think together. It is not accidental that when the problematic togetherness between the true and the good is dismantled by articulating them clearly and distinctly in their apartness, the result is the disappearance of the soul as the fundamental object of human inquiry.

In the late 1980's Kennington gave a lecture entitled "Final Causality and Modern Natural Right" in which he suggested that the distinction between ancients and moderns turns on the question of teleology. The anti-teleological ire of the moderns, the deepest version of their anti-theological ire, has a Machiavellian root that rejects teleology in the human sphere and a Baconian root that rejects teleology in the non-human sphere. The two seem akin but in fact are hard to put together, for science does not spring full-blown from the head of Zeus but is rather a human project that must be understood in terms of a purpose or end. Early modern philosophy is plagued by this problem – the need to provide a *telos* for its anti-teleological program. It is the genuine dualism of which the mind/body problem is but a pale reflection.

Modernity's attack on teleology is directed ultimately at ancient philosophy. To understand it Kennington looks back at ancient teleologies and discovers three types: universal teleology, moral teleology, and the teleology of the philosophic life – what he calls Socratic teleology. Universal teleology, the most obvious target of the moderns, has a very uncertain role within ancient thought; it is openly problematic in Plato (*Phaedo* 96b ff.) and even if one does not accept that it is only exoterically unproblematic in Aristotle, it is certainly unnecessary for, and even at odds with, his moral teleology – his ranking of lives. Moral teleology, in turn, points to the natural teleology of intellectual virtue without supplying the natural ground for moral virtue. Accordingly, ancient philosophy, whether Platonic or Aristotelian, finally seems confident of only one form of teleology – the goodness of the philosophic or contemplative life, which, ironically, would be impossible in a world in which the universal teleology prevailed. Socratic teleology is confirmed by our experience that the good is not good unless it is real or true, and that there is a certain satisfaction in the truth even when it runs contrary to our desires. But, as Professor McCarthy suggests, this experience of the togetherness of the good and the true is only available to us in a world in which they are apart.

Why then is Kennington so interested in modern philosophy, in which we find what he calls "the typically modern paradox. . . : what is good is not known to be true, and what is true is not known to be good"?[6] Here I am in a way grateful that, unlike Professors Velkley and McCarthy, I am only commenting and have the luxury of speculating without the burden of proving. Kennington says of Francis Bacon that he "clearly . . . wants us to rethink the first attempt [of the ancients – the attempt to find what is absolutely prior in the order of nature], so that the second sailing, the relapse into final causality will be unnecessary."[7] In other words, Bacon sends us back to re-examine the pre-Socratics. Similarly, "Without full self-consciousness of its necessity, [Descartes] was compelled to repeat in part the Socratic discovery of the *terra incognita*, the human experience of the human.[8] In hyperbolically separating the true from the

6 "The 'Teaching of Nature' in Descartes' Soul Doctrine," 116.
7 "Final Causality and Modern Natural Right,"15.
8 "The 'Teaching of Nature' in Descartes' Soul Doctrine," 117.

good, and in struggling with the problem of their recombination, modern philosophy makes visible in a particularly powerful form the shape of the human soul. As Nietzsche once claimed of those he called modern psychologists, they are more interesting than their doctrines. In their dismantling of the human soul, the early modern philosophers make the human soul especially manifest. It is perhaps only a small exaggeration to say that what the pre-Socratic philosophers were to Socrates, the early moderns were to Richard Kennington. His particular concern might then be understood to be either the question "Who is the philosopher?", or the relation between the true and the good, or perhaps the question of teleology. At the root of all of these, however, it seems to me is the question of the human soul. Kennington's life-long preoccupation with it may account for the impression he invariably left of unfathomable depth.

Chapter 16

SETH BENARDETE:
THE LIFE OF WONDER[1]

There were certain times in Benardete's classes when questions would uncharacteristically break out. On one particular evening in a course on the *Phaedo* in the spring of 1980 (it seems so much more recent than that), David O'Brien first asked Benardete what we were going to do when he died, to which Seth gave a silent but expressive shrug. In a follow up Mr. O'Brien asked whether it didn't make Seth angry that he would die, To this he replied, "No, I have always considered it a privilege to have lived." Now, as with many of the things Seth said, this beautiful remark is both striking and illusive, especially in light of something else he once said. Having begun a sentence with "It has always seemed to me . . . ," Seth stopped abruptly and added "My brother, José, has noticed that whenever someone says 'It has always seemed to me,' about something, it invariably means that he has just thought of it." Perhaps this was true of his view of life as a privilege for which one ought to be grateful, not a right violated by the uncanny certainty of death; still this view is consistent with his much later "Platonic reading" of the *Odyssey*, and especially with his interpretation of the passage read a moment

1 Originally given on February 1, 2002 at New York University at a memorial service for Seth Benardete.

ago. Odysseus the man of mind refuses immortality because he understands that there is no mind without soul, and no soul without death. This is perhaps the deepest version of what Seth called the teleology of evil. To learn one must experience or suffer – *pathei mathos*. This suffering must remain hard, but knowledge of its necessity somehow transforms it. Because to be alive means to die, to be angry about the fact of death means to hate life. Seth was a lover of life, which was for him the love of learning – philosophy.

Seth was first a figure of gossip for me. During a year at Heidelberg, I read Plato's *Philebus* with Tom Schmid and Richard Velkley. Schmid, who I think had heard Seth lecture at Yale, gave an elaborate description of what he called his "magnificent head." Later I would always put this together with the dark brooding photograph at the beginning of Seth's essay on Greek tragedy. The outside does not always reflect the inside, but Seth's looks reflected his *eidos* – at once daunting and seductive. When I decided to do my dissertation on the *Philebus*, Richard Kennington, my advisor, made available to me Seth's course notes on the dialogue. I had looked at most of the literature and had just finished a seminar on the *Philebus* with Hans-Georg Gadamer, but all that was nothing compared to Benardete. He had an uncanny ability to see the profundity lying concealed on the surface of things. Once one understood that the Greek expression *kata noun* (to my mind) meant "pleasing," it was clear that in the very first sentence of the *Philebus* Plato had already denied the separation of mind and pleasure which is the dialogue's putative theme. The truth of *kata noun* is that there is no mind without desire, without soul.

At Kennington's urging, I sent Seth a copy of my finished dissertation. He wrote back within the fortnight – he had "read it with pleasure, for it [was] very well written" . . . and then "indeed, too well written given the matter discussed." There followed pages of intricate criticism which I had the humbling experience of simply not understanding. Rereading it many years later, I began to see what he had had in mind when he spoke of the relation between eros and mind. But at the time I was perplexed, disappointed, and a little angry – superficially at him, really at myself. Over the years I saw others respond as I had. It is difficult to discover someone who knows what you are supposed to know so much better than you know it. And Seth didn't make it easier, for it was a point of principle with him to converse with others as though they shared his unconditional devotion to getting at the truth of things. He always treated interlocutors as equals, and it was always a lie, for he was the intellectual superior of everyone with whom I ever heard him converse. But by way of this noble lie he made us better than ourselves.

For years I sat in on his classes at the New School and at NYU – the first a seminar on Sophocles' *Philoctetes* in the fall of 1979. It started at 6:10 and usually lasted until 10:30. Then we would go out afterward, to the Cedar Tavern, or in later years to Homer's Diner. Sometimes there were several of us; sometimes he and I were alone. The conversation was like nothing I had before experienced. It would usually start with unresolved puzzles generated in the class, then turn to politics or the newest problem in cosmology. We might talk about Heidegger and Strauss. Or we might discuss whatever he was reading – the memoirs of Babur, the Great Mogul of the 16th century, or of Mildred Cable, a Christian missionary to Mongolia. Or we might talk about Tibetan grammar, or Patricia Cornwell, or his interpretation of *Star Wars*, *The Wizard of Oz*, Rome, Christianity, Judaism, Cervantes, the *Arabian Nights*, Hades, and at one point or another every figure in the history of philosophy. And of course there was Plato, for Seth the measure of everyone else, and tragedy, the question to which he always returned. His conversation danced with ease over an enormous range but was somehow never superficial. It was most exhilarating when we circled back to put together these odd pieces into a single whole. Seth and I used to joke about how strange it was that in any given semester the different books we were teaching ended up being about the same thing. One day during that first year I was walking to my office with one of my students. Intelligent and yet a little presumptuous (as Sarah Lawrence students are wont to be), she asked me what had happened. I didn't know what she meant. Well, she said, I had been a pretty good teacher the previous year, but something had changed, something in the way I looked at things, I was somehow more alive. She couldn't quite put her finger on it, but she assured me that I had somehow – well – changed. I could put my finger on it; I had met Seth Benardete.

After the Cedar Tavern, when Seth walked me to the subway; the conversation would return to what he had talked about in class. I don't know how many times I had to race through Grand Central Station to catch the last train of the night back to White Plains. I would get home at 2:30 or so, get to bed by three, and the telephone would ring. Without so much as a hello, Benardete's voice would say "I've just discovered this beautiful thing" and the conversation would continue from where we had left off. In later years we would walk from Homer's to my car; then I would drive him home. On one bitterly cold night we sat for two hours on 12th Street. The conversation had gone back and forth all evening on *Republic*, Book 3. Seth interrupted himself in midsentence and in that excited breathy tone said "Wait, wait, wait. . . . Could it possibly be . . . ?" He had discovered the connection between the *kalon*, the beautiful, and *thumos*, spiritedness, that would prove so crucial for his book, *Socrates' Second Sailing*. I thought about what he had said all the way home – somehow it was now "our" discovery. That night too I got a call. While I had been delighting in "our" discovery, Seth had already reformulated it and pushed it to another level. The following week in class, I had expected to see it triumphantly hauled out for display, but he had transformed it still further so that it was no longer altogether recognizable to me. His books too read like this; most authors pause to sum up what they have accomplished. Seth's writings are so difficult not because any sentence is particularly opaque, but because of the collective weight that must be borne when every sentence adds something important. He so delighted in discovery because it enabled him to discover still more. The entire world was the object of his wonder – himself only insofar as he was an example of the most peculiar part of it.

I first saw Benardete at a memorial for Leo Strauss, and the first words I heard him utter were "Leo Strauss was a philosopher." Seth never claimed to be a philosopher; he knew the danger of supplanting love of wisdom by love of self. But honesty requires us now to call him that. Drew Keller once asked him if he still thought about Strauss, to which he responded, "every day." Benardete used to tell a story about the public presentation of his Master's thesis on the *Theages* at the University of Chicago. As he was reading it, he periodically heard giggling from behind him – where the members of his committee were seated. Afterward Strauss came up to him and said "I didn't know you were such a funny man." No one else had got the joke. Benardete was the most playful and the most profound man I ever met; in him the two were one. It must surely have been difficult for him that even those of us who admired him most had only a glimmer of their togetherness.

For twenty-two years it was my privilege to share in a conversation that, however staggeringly broad its range, was still one conversation – an on-going attempt (in which nothing was too petty to be considered) to glimpse the true pieces of the world in their mutual connection. Having tasted the sweetness of this conversation, it is hard to imagine life without it, and yet hard as well to imagine it without him, so thoroughly have thinking and talking to Benardete come to mean the same thing for me. Knowing him – being his student and later his friend – has been the great gift of my life.

Seth generally indulged but did not share my admiration for certain contemporary authors – Saul Bellow, Tom Stoppard, and others. I would like to conclude by reading a passage from one of them – a poet whom Seth thought interesting, but not that interesting, Wallace Stevens. Nevertheless, as this part of a poem called "The Sail of Ulysses" seems to me particularly appropriate, I will ask his indulgence this one last time.

> If knowledge and the thing known are one
> So that to know a man is to be
> That man, to know a place is to be
> That place, and it seems to come to that;

And if to know one man is to know all
And if one's sense of a single spot
Is what one knows of the universe,
Then knowledge is the only life,
The only sun of the only day,
The only access to true ease,
The deep comfort of the world and fate.[2]

2   Stevens, Wallace, "The Sail of Ulysses," in *Opus Posthumus* (New York: Knopf, 1972), 99-100.

Chapter 17

A LIFE OF LEARNING[1]

First, thanks a lot for inviting me; it is an honor that those of you who have studied with me actually want to hear more – and not even for credit. Let me start with a puzzle. Most of you were born in the year I began teaching at Sarah Lawrence; so I've been here for rather a long time. Why then do I still feel like one of the new people, one of the young Turks who just arrived – twenty-one years ago? A related puzzle: I've had a beard since 1971, but when I get up in the morning and look in the mirror, I'm always a little surprised by it. So why do I expect the face of a seventeen-year-old to stare back at me?

Euripides wrote a play called the *Helen*. According to the plot, Helen never went to Troy with Paris; she was replaced by a phantom image fashioned by Hera out of air. The real Helen was whisked away to Egypt. As the play opens Helen identifies herself to us and, of course, we have to accept her word – that's what you do when you watch a play. Still, in another context the whole thing would be problematic. The two Helens are so alike that neither Menelaus, who has spent the last seven years with the phantom, nor Paris, who lived with her for ten years, know that she is not real. And, of course, the event that defines the Greeks as Greek – the Trojan War – was fought for the phantom. Now, were you a little cynical, you might

1   Originally the 1999 Senior Lecture at Sarah Lawrence College.

say "Isn't that just like men?"; still, what does it mean for the one who remained in Egypt to be the real Helen? What does our identity really consist in?

The *Helen* begins with a series of images that emphasize the split between motion and rest. Put these two together, and you get the gods who are always the same in their role as paradigms (love, war, sky, earth, etc.) and nevertheless, as alive – as persons – are always changing (Ares may mean war and Aphrodite beauty, but they also sleep together, to the consternation of Aphrodite's husband, Hephaestus, and the amusement and titillation of the rest of the gods). This is connected to the issue that dominates the *Helen* and almost makes it a comedy: nobody recognizes anybody else in this play. When Teucer, a Greek veteran of the war, comes to Egypt, he sees Helen and is amazed that there could be such a look-alike for the "real" Helen. Menelaus, shipwrecked and in rags, is upset that the old woman porter at the door of the king of Egypt does not recognize him for what he is. When he hears that there is a woman named Helen who lives in the house, he speculates that perhaps there is in Egypt a parallel world where there is even another man named Zeus. When Helen and Menelaus first meet, she does not recognize him even though she has been told that he is in Egypt, and he does not recognize her until he has been told by a messenger that the phantom Helen has vanished. The messenger at first thinks that Helen is the re-appearance of the phantom Helen, whom he, of course, takes to be the real Helen. The connection between the togetherness of motion and rest and recognition emerges in the most puzzling line of the play. In the scene we have all been waiting for, where Helen and Menelaus eventually recognize each other, she first runs from him thinking he is one of her captors. He is struck by her face, but she seems not to be sure who he is. While she knows who he is supposed to be, she can't believe her eyes and says "O gods! For even to recognize friends is a god." At first we think she has recognized him and is grateful, but the recognition doesn't come until several lines later. So, here Helen seems to mean instead that it is as difficult to recognize even those closest and most dear to you as it is to recognize a god. Menelaus has aged in the seventeen years since she last saw him, and she cannot be sure who he is. It is as difficult to grasp the unchanging core of another human being as it is to recognize a god. The gods in their double being as constant (or at rest) and changing (or in motion) are simply bolder versions of the problem of human identity. We are at once the same as we were when we were born (or when we were 17) and yet constantly changing and so never really the same at all. We grow and learn, become happy and bitter, graduate and teach at Sarah Lawrence, and so on. The *Helen* literally splits Helen at the beginning into her name – i.e., her phantom – and her body in Egypt. The name goes to Troy, and the result is *the* story of Helen and Menelaus, a story that necessarily holds them in some sense constant so that its motion is intelligible. Helen *is* "the face that launched a thousand ships," and Menelaus *is* the sacker of Troy. The real Helen, who presumably changes, goes to Egypt, which Euripides likens to Hades and so suggests is a place where nothing changes. What is peculiar about the play, then, is that in order to show us the difference between the name which hides Helen's reality by stabilizing her and Helen's reality, Euripides must tell another story about Helen, which of course necessarily treats her as in some way constant.

You could put the general problem this way. To identify something is to name it – to tag it, put a seal on it, or put it to rest. But what does it mean to do that to a human being? *The* being that has as its being to be in motion is the soul. In Greek the word for name – *onoma* – is the same as the word for noun. Can one really turn a verb into a noun in this way? Can one be expected, for example, to talk about a *life* of learning and one's own life to boot? Have you asked me to do the impossible today as a sort of perverse revenge because I have so often given you impossible paper topics? Maybe I should change the emphasis of my very first sentence: Thanks a *lot* for inviting me.

Still, Helen pulls it off; she identifies herself by telling her story. And then Euripides tells a larger story about how she comes to do so. Stories – *muthoi* – are what they are by putting together rest and motion. So maybe I will tell a few stories, and with any luck, something of my identity will get through.

But not yet; first, Aristotle. There is really more at stake here than whether I mess up the Senior Lecture. The first book of Aristotle's *Nicomachean Ethics* is about happiness. Can we call anyone happy who has not experienced a complete life? Aristotle is thinking of Solon's famous remark that we should count no man happy until his is dead and so is indirectly reminding us of Solon's other famous saying that as he grows older he constantly learns many things. You can see the connection. Suppose wisdom is the source of happiness. If you are always learning something new, and if everything is connected to everything else, then you never really know what you think you know, you are not really wise, and so cannot really be happy. In his version of this problem of human happiness, Aristotle calls our attention to the life of Priam of Troy to attest to the dangers of premature judgment. No matter that you have fared very well for most of your life, if in your last days, your sons are killed, your wife and daughters raped, and the city over which you have ruled long and prosperously is ransacked and burned. It looks as though either one can never count oneself happy, or one could do so only if there were a place like Hades from which a judgment of one's life as a whole could be made after death. Here Aristotle makes a rather queer digression about whether the dead in Hades can be made unhappy by the shameful deeds of their living relations – you thought you were happy but your great granddaughter gets caught shoplifting after you are dead. It all seems quite bizarre until one realizes what is at stake – the possibility of a perspective from which one can judge one's life which is at the same time immune from the incomplete and precarious nature of life as it is lived. Hades looks to be absurd. Either you do not live on, in which case there is no vantage point from which to judge your life, and your life is never experienced as complete; or else you do live on, in which case you can still be affected by things and your life is never experienced as complete. Hades is simply graduate school. In either case you will never be able to count yourself happy, and so will never be able to be happy in any final sense. You cannot say "I am happy" because the "I" does not remain constant; this is not an accident of your particular life; it is rather inherent in the very character of what it means to be a self in the world. Life is by its very nature incomplete and incompletable.

Sorry, maybe we should talk about my childhood in upstate New York (like Priam and Paris, I come from Troy). Ok, but first, Rousseau. The third of his *Reveries of the Solitary Walker* begins with an epigraph – a familiar quotation from Solon: "I come to be old, while always learning." Rousseau laments this fact for reasons very like the ones we have seen. It looks as though learning always comes too late. Because we can never grasp our lives as wholes, we learn to live only after it is not of any use to us. Learning means discovering potentially terrible mistakes – mistakes perhaps without remedy. To avoid this situation, Rousseau decides that when he is forty, he will consider himself a completed work, simply adopt whatever views seem to him most likely, and live faithfully, and guiltlessly, for the remainder of his life using them as moral standards. Of course this is preposterous, and he knows it; Rousseau writes the *Reveries* when he is in his sixties and in the very next one, the fourth, tells us that the day before yesterday he meditated about whether lying was ever moral. So apparently his fixed moral principles are under constant revision. Still, we are meant to learn something about the structure of morality from this phantom stability. To be a moral being means regularly to jump outside of oneself to take stock of oneself as a whole. We may not know how it is possible for us to take this measure of our lives, but our everyday experiences of duty and obligation suggest that we are nevertheless doing it all the time. Rousseau placed the quotation of Solon over the third reverie as an epigraph to signal what it was about as a whole. Apparently it is possible to have sufficient distance on ourselves to know that it is our nature never simply to be complete. This is self-consciousness – in its double sense of self-awareness and embarrassment. We capture ourselves in our awareness that we are always in motion.

Stories. I was born in a log cabin. That's not true, of course, but it is not as far from true as you might think. I was actually born in Albany, New York. My parents met in their mid-twenties and in the century's mid-thirties working in Gimbels Department Store in New York City. It wasn't long before they were caught up in trying to unionize the store (the International Ladies Garment Workers Union) and it wasn't long afterward that they became members of the American Communist Party. When the war broke out, my father joined the Navy; they taught him to be a radar technician and then, because he had unreliable political views, sent him to San Clemente Island, California, where he spent three years manning the radar station and diving for abalone. After the war, the Party sent my parents to upstate New York to organize labor unions. My father got a job in Troy shoveling coal at a non-union factory – working the night shift so that he could do his real work during the day. I was born at about this time. Their story is actually much more interesting than mine, but to make it short, they lost their faith, decided to leave the Party and, attempted to walk an impossible line between cooperating with federal investigators and withholding specific information about men and women who had been their friends for fifteen years. When it was all over they had no friends, and so decided to light out for the territory. They bought a half-acre of land in rural West Sand Lake, New York, about ten miles from Troy.

Here's where I come in. This was in the spring of 1951; I was three. They bought an army surplus tent; my father cleared the land of trees (with an axe, not a chainsaw), and there we were – two adults and three small children in a tent on a piece of land that abutted the swampy end of a little lake. A log cabin would have been a luxury. My father had to build some kind of shelter for us in the five months before winter set in. The funny thing is that he had never built anything before in his life. But he had all he needed – inexhaustible optimism and the ability to read. I still have the *Home Handyman's Guide* that he gave me when, having come to Sarah Lawrence, my wife and I found ourselves in a similar, if less dire, situation. The cost of living in Westchester County meant that we could only afford a house quaintly described as a "handyman's special" but in reality pretty much a wreck. Anyway, this very book had taught him how to talk about building, and so how to ask questions without being laughed at. It also guided him to other books that actually taught him how to build. We were lucky as well. Down the road from us. (It was a dirt road that would have had weeds growing

in a line down the center were it not for the oil the town poured on
it every summer to keep the dust down. One of my strongest mem-
ories from that time is walking down this road hand in hand with my
sisters to the part of the lake where you could swim; the oil was hot
on our bare feet, and did not come off so easily.) . . . Anyway, about
a half-mile down this road lived a man who had an old ice-house he
wanted to take down so that he could build a garage. My father
offered to help him deconstruct it if he could keep the ice house.
First he removed the roof and then detached the four walls from one
another so that they collapsed atop each other into a square. Then he
made a sort of harness fastened in turn to each of the walls and
hitched it over his shoulders. One by one he dragged the walls to our
little plot of land and then reassembled the whole. Over the years,
our house would grow in all sorts of quirky ways, but to this day Mr.
Cumming's ice-house is at its core. Shortly after this, my father
bought an old yellow car, cut off the top in back, and turned it into
a truck (later when it would run no longer, he cut the truck in half
and made a trailer). He used both to haul building materials bought
second-hand from sites where old buildings were being torn down
to make way for new construction. The living room he eventually
built for this house was about twenty feet square with two adjacent
walls completely windowed from floor to ceiling and overlooking
our swamp. The house was filled with wonderful details like this.
On the other hand, there was scarcely a right angle to be found in it;
learning by doing has its glorious side, but it also has its limitations.

I've spent so much time on this on the one hand because I enjoy
thinking about it, but also because I learned from it the great power
of intelligence and the enormous fun involved in its exercise. By
inclination, but also by necessity, my father's view of the world
around him, of its possibilities and limitations, was remarkably free
of conventional expectations. He was not really a part of this world
he had stumbled into, and being apart from it had enabled him to
come to it in a curiously fresh way. I like to think this is an image of
the fixed principle of the motion of my own life. My parents were
city folk and former communists, she a Jew who grew up in a family of Yiddish actors and he the non-believing son of a freemason

and a Christian Scientist. They found themselves in rural, conservative, Christian upstate New York. And they liked it. Over the years they became increasingly involved in the community, but without being resentful, they never lost sight of the fact that they were strangers in a strange land. Because they got in the habit of thinking of ordinary things as strange, they were at home with the strangeness of the world. It is impossible for me to describe them without running headlong into the inadequacies of my own descriptive talents. For many years, on the first day of spring my father would march his children around the backyard with pots and pans and spoons to bang on them – to welcome in spring, he said. To understand him you need to know that there was never anything saccharine about this; it was more like a pagan rite, more an ironic philosophic wonder than flower-childishness.

Eventually I inherited this sense of alienation from them, but with an added wrinkle – I don't feel at home in the city either. At first though, I had no idea that we were peculiar. I had a rather idyllic pre-adolescence – playing Vikings on the lake in an old wooden boat, catching frogs, playing baseball, and reading. My mother's notion of the classics was wonderfully inclusive – anything old that people had once liked. So I read Jack London, Sinclair Lewis, Mark Twain, and (my own addition) Chip Hilton Sports Stories. One Christmas I received as a gift a beautiful complete hardbound set of Dickens. Of course, it wasn't really complete. My mother had gotten it for two dollars at a used book store; it was so inexpensive because it was missing all of the best known novels. I am probably the only person alive who thinks of Charles Dickens primarily as the author of *Martin Chuzzlewit* and *Barnaby Rudge*. Needless to say my taste developed in a totally chaotic way. My parents were great but they didn't know anything about books, and I never seemed to run into anyone who did (years later, during a college vacation, I went to the local bookstore in Troy – Lavender's – and asked what they had by Plato; they asked me for his first name).

I was good at school, but altogether unselfconsciously. Then things started to change. At the beginning of the Fourth Book of *Emile*, Rousseau says that we are each born twice – once for our species and once for our sex. Sex forces you to look at yourself through the eyes of an imagined other; you desire and so want to be desired. Wanting to be noticed means noticing oneself. This leads to an increased sense of the conditions governing your own existence and so willy nilly of your own mortality. Love and death have a way of making themselves felt even in upstate New York. People respond differently, of course. I am sure I knew I was going to die before I was a teenager; nevertheless I remember waking up in a cold sweat on the night that it actually sank in. Or, maybe not; maybe I had been reading *Crime and Punishment*. In either case, I remember coming to a resolution: whatever I did would matter; it would be the very best thing I could do with my life. What I experienced that night has been called our "ontological honor." All living things die; we are privileged to know in advance that we will die. This awareness of our own finitude places an enormous burden on us. We have to choose what we will do with our lives and accordingly are in one way or another compelled to ask the question "What is the best life?"

Now, an infinite threat tends to call forth an infinite response. Death first frightens you and then insults you. You get angry and devise ways to combat it. In the short term, my pretty unsophisticated response to death's insult was to resolve to do everything, as though I were compiling the complete human resume to impress God. So I threw myself into sports, and school, and drama and lots of other things. But a part of me knew that this refusal to choose would not do in the long term. I wanted to find a choice that would allow me in some way to have it all. There seemed to my naïve soul to be two possibilities: politics, because it somehow dealt with everything, and physics, because it somehow dealt with everything. Had I been able to think through the meaning of my political longings, I would have seen that, like Plato's *Glaucon*, I really aspired to universal tyranny – "to be the universal beloved of all mankind." But, while my parents had been communists, I was thoroughly bourgeois; I thought I wanted to be president. On the other hand there was physics. Mine was the Sputnik generation when physicists had suddenly become national heroes. But my theoretical bent simply concealed another form of the longing to be the universal beloved of all mankind, for if everyone else thinks you have lived the absolutely best life mustn't it be true? Had I been less innocent, I might have added a few alternatives. Had I known, for example, that "the poets are the unacknowledged legislators of the world," I might have wanted to be an author. And had I known then of the ancient quarrel between philosophy and poetry, I might have wanted to be a philosopher. But no matter what I had thought I wanted, its reality would have been the longing for recognition.

Now despite my various high school triumphs, the guidance counselors didn't seem to know that, however polite and well behaved, I was still a destiny. I told them I wanted to apply to Cornell; they told me not to be silly (no one from my school had ever done that) and that I should go to a local college. Fortunately, I had inherited certain traits, impracticality, inexhaustible optimism (and the ability to read books); so, ignoring little difficulties like how the son of TV serviceman was going to pay for all of this, I applied to Cornell and got a scholarship. Life at Cornell was interesting. The rooms had right angles and, at the time, maid service and clean linens every week. And there were people there from prep schools; I scarcely knew what a prep school was. Most of the people in my freshman dormitory seemed to feel as though they were camping out – on temporary furlough from real life; to me it all felt like a luxury hotel. Now, on the one hand I didn't quite fit; people knew a lot more than I did – what calculus was for example. On the other hand, this place was clearly invented for me. But my master plan – physics and politics – wasn't in such good shape. I wasn't all that good at physics and waiting tables had taught me that I didn't much like being constantly judged on how I was serving people. The illogic of defining the best life as recognition from those to whom one fought to be superior had just about turned itself into nihilism when I encountered a truly remarkable man who changed my life – Allan Bloom.

Bloom wasn't yet famous (he hadn't written *The Closing of the American Mind*, and so becoming the *bête noire* of the academic world was still in his future), but he was an extraordinary teacher. At first I didn't really understand what he was saying. It was enough that his love of the books he taught was palpable. He was wickedly witty and very good at making students feel the paradox of their non-judgmental self-righteousness. But he was never cruel. He lured us into perplexities only to make us long for the truth. Then he would tell us that the only reason to read old books was the hope that you might find the truth in them. He never underestimated the difficulty of discovering the truth and never claimed to have it, but that only made the search more alluring. He was a world class apologist for philosophy which he understood, following his teacher Leo Strauss, on the basis of a wonderful sentence in Pascal's *Penseés*: "We know too little to be dogmatists and too much to be skeptics." For the first time I began to get an inkling that a way of life might be possible that did not attempt to overcome death, but rather understood it and the alienation it implies as a condition necessary for everything that is good in human life – our ontological honor. A human being is the only part of the whole that is open to the whole, but this openness is only possible because of a certain detachment from the whole, a certain alienation. The possibility of knowledge is thus purchased at the price of the impossibility of complete knowledge.

But all of this was still in the future for me. At first, I saw in philosophy only another way to do everything – the choice of choices. I asked Bloom to be my advisor – he taught in the Government Department, so I became a Government major. Now, you can take the boy out of West Sand Lake, but you cannot take West Sand Lake out of the boy. So, because I took Bloom's praise of the philosophical life so seriously, in my trusting way I immediately went off to register in the philosophy department, where I would later take a double major. I had no idea that Cornell had at the time one of the pre-eminent analytic philosophy departments in the country – that they did not even acknowledge what Bloom was doing to be philosophy and that he returned their contempt in kind. They hated each other, but I wanted to be a philosopher. Where else would one go but the philosophy department?

I was lucky again. Bloom was such a seductive teacher, and one must admit that a certain cultishness developed around him and, perhaps, more importantly, around his teacher, Leo Strauss. At the risk of making complicated things much too simple, Strauss had seen that questions of truth are inseparable from moral questions, that ancient philosophers tended to be more attuned to and less skeptical of this connection than moderns, that such truth as is available to us is at best only very indirectly known and articulated, and that accordingly genuine philosophers have tended to practice an art of writing designed to reveal what they mean only indirectly. Wrench any of these insights from the others and Strauss can easily appear to be a moral dogmatist, a romantic who idealizes life in the Greek *polis*, or a perverse interpreter and elitist bent on the discovery of secret teachings available only to the few. Students, of course, are simultaneously attracted to and repelled by dogmatism, romanticism, idealism, perversity, and elitism – vices to which Straussians sometimes succumb. But having enrolled in the anti-Bloom, anti-Strauss, philosophy department, I had a sort of inoculation against these excesses. At the same time, Bloom kept me honest in the battle against the parallel seduction in the philosophy department – Ludwig Wittgenstein. So once more I was in the strange position of being simultaneously inside and out. The people in the philosophy department thought I was a little "off"; how could you trust someone who read Nietzsche? Bloom, on the other hand, could never understand what on earth I found interesting in Wittgenstein.

Now, all of this competition was exhilarating, but it was really a sign that I had not understood anything yet. Philosophy was still for me too much the pot at the end of the rainbow, El Dorado, and the Holy Grail. At the end of Plato's *Symposium* the drunken Alcibiades gives an account of Socrates after the battle of Potidaea standing in the snow for twenty-four hours straight looking up at the heavens in philosophical contemplation. But this is Alcibiades' view of philosophy, not Plato's. Plato's Socrates is much more likely to show his true nature in the give and take of conversation. I think I finally learned this when Bloom, on leave for a semester, arranged for Richard Kennington to teach in his place. Kennington taught philosophy at Penn State. At Cornell he gave a seminar on Descartes, and for the first time I saw someone enacting what Bloom had been so seductively advertising. Here was a man so utterly losing himself in thinking, in figuring out what a text and the world to which it referred meant, that I could imagine how the being who is open to the whole could take its deepest fulfillment in the contemplation of the whole. I could imagine how the philosophical life could be not a trophy to be won and displayed but a life to be lived.

When I told my advisor in the philosophy department that I was studying with the man Allan Bloom said knew more about Descartes than anyone in the world (Bloom was never shy of hyperbole), he asked me his name. "Richard Kennington," I said. He looked him up in the *Directory of American Philosophers* and discovered that at about age 50, he was only an instructor. He had never finished his dissertation. That might have deterred someone who hadn't known my father, but I had already made plans to begin graduate work at Penn State the following year. People like Kennington were too rare to pass up. After all, I had inexhaustible optimism, and I knew how to read.

Now you no doubt are beginning to wonder where this will all end. So, let's put a stop to it. I taught briefly at three other places before I came to Sarah Lawrence in 1977, but I feel as though my whole life was a preparation for it. In a college where politics tend to be a little to the left of Che Guevera, I think I probably appear somewhere a little to the right of Genghis Khan. Where what is most prized is what is newest and most creative, and the old is looked at with considerable suspicion, I unapologetically teach the old. But the fact remains, and I am always a little surprised at it: they pay me to do this. At times it can be alienating, but properly understood alienation is a great good disguising itself as an unmixed evil. To be sure, we feel the loss when irony moderates our enthusiasms, but we need always to remember that by doing so it keeps us in touch with our deeper selves. From a distance, alienation is our greatest consolation.

INDEX